First & Last Editions

England's Second-Hand Bookshops

Contents

Acknowledgements

The Author gratefully acknowledges permission to reproduce the following pictures:

Cover picture Richard Lannoy's painting of the Camden Bookshop in Bath

Pages 4 & 5 Ken Spelman's bookshop in Micklegate, York

Page 9 Hall's bookshop in Tunbridge Wells

Page 12 The Arundel Bookshop

Page 36 Camilla's, Eastbourne

Page 41 Sanctuary Bookshop, Lyme Regis

Introduction

They say you can tell a man's character and inclinations from the books on his shelves. If that is so, then it seems to me as I look along mine in their coats of many colours that they portray me pretty accurately, even allowing for the fact that I have what amounts to another small library five hundred miles distant in Aberdeen, my birthplace. Put the two collections together and the result would probably be a marginal change of emphasis here and there between the various categories and subjects; but essentially the same person is revealed.

Judged by the contents of the Carshalton shelves, he has a strong but highly selective interest in sport, with rugby union, cricket and bowls foremost, and the odd place allowed to football and golf. There are biographies and autobiographies from Bernard Shaw to Alan Ross; a dozen volumes by W. H. Hudson, greatest of naturalists; travels with Henry James and Paul Theroux and Edwin Muir; books on cinema Westerns; essays by Ford Madox Ford and Edward Thomas; a novel or two; and a little poetry. The bulk of these books, as you may notice, are dependent, to a greater or lesser extent, on fact, suggesting, correctly, that their owner is a journalist.

This book, which is a mixture of fact, anecdote and quotation, describes my meandering exploration of some of the best of England's provincial second-hand bookshops, from Newcastle-upon-Tyne to the Isles of Scilly. It is not a directory and I have made no attempt to divide it into areas – north, south-east, and so on. Some pieces deal with a single shop, others with one outstanding shop and two or three lesser ones. And by shop I mean shop: I have omitted businesses described as "private premises; appointment necessary."

If you like supermarkets for books as well as for food, Waterstone's and Dillon's will be sufficient for you. But there are no surprises in Waterstone's and Dillon's, just as there are no surprises in Sainsbury's, and without that element of surprise searching for books loses half its pleasure. There were many surprises during the eighteen-month journey that follows.

Traylen's

I started at Guildford. Traylen's occupies Castle House in Quarry Street, at the foot of the High Street, on land that once formed part of the castle grounds. Since the sixteenth century it has been, variously, a residence for assize judges, a boys' school, a private house, and furniture galleries. Not far away is the house where Lewis Carroll died.

Charles Traylen, who served his apprenticeship in the antiquarian book business in Cambridge in the 1920s, set up on his own in Guildford in 1945, moving to Quarry Street in 1959. "I began with a dozen shelves of books and a mortgage," he says. *Drif's*, that eccentric, readable guide to second-hand bookshops, describes Traylen's as "solid roast beef", meaning that it is "a bookshop which is attempting to sell the same books as were popular fifty years ago." That, as it happens, is roughly how long ago Traylen's was founded, in the last year of the war. Has Traylen's, then, failed to move with the times? Then again, is it an essential function of such shops to move with the times at all, given that they deal in non-current merchandise? I have my doubts.

Anyway, I liked Traylen's very much. It has a large stock distributed through twenty-and-odd rooms, and you can browse away happily, upstairs and downstairs, without tripping over piles of unplaced books, knowing that things will be in sensible order and not thrown together too haphazardly.

Classics and children's books were on adjacent shelves in a corner of the ground floor. I noted nearly twenty volumes of E. V. Lucas's essays, a staple of second-hand bookshops; and, in the children's section, some authors' names familiar from my boyhood: Biggles's creator W. E. Johns, F. S. Brereton, Percy F. Westerman, R. M. Ballantyne and Douglas V. Duff, but no G. A. Henty. This was a surprise, but in any case I had never liked Henty, whose style I thought as heavy as the bindings of his books, with their history-lesson titles such as *Under Wellington's Command* and *With Roberts to Pretoria.*

Something called *A Modern Chronicle*, by Winston Churchill, published in 1910 and evidently neither a classic nor a children's book, had strayed into this corner, and for an incredible moment I wondered whether it was an unknown novel by the Churchill of Churchills. But according to a pencilled note on the inner front cover, the author was an American novelist of the same name who lived from 1871 to 1947, and a glance at any page confirmed the book's provenance.

This Guildford visit, my second, ended with a pleasant surprise. Leaving Traylen's I walked on an impulse to the top of the High Street, looked into Thomas Thorp's shop, and in the second-hand department asked if they stocked *The Book Browser's Guide*, by Roy Harley Lewis, which I had placed with booksearchers at Leatherhead the previous week after learning of its existence from Traylen's. The assistant walked straight to a bottom shelf and brought forth a copy for me.

Stone Trough, York

On our way to York on a Sunday morning we stopped for lunch at Stamford and explored the bookshop on St Mary's Hill, which has one of the biggest collections of cricket books I have seen, including numerous *Wisdens*, probably worth a lot. "We answer requests from all over the world," the lady behind the counter told us. Beekeeping and campanology are among the shop's specialities; there were stuffed birds on display; and you could buy ice cream and newspapers. But none of these peripheral things seemed to distract the public's attention from the shelves.

Then on to York, a city of gates. Starting at the Minster, High Petergate goes down into Low Petergate, which in turn becomes Colliergate, before you enter Fossgate, York's miniature Charing Cross Road, with more bookshops than you could find in many a large town. Stone Trough Books is at number thirty-eight, sharing premises with Philip Martin's music shop.

George Ramsden, an Etonian, runs Stone Trough, so named because his family had a brewery in Halifax called Stone Trough. After experience with Heywood Hill in Mayfair, he opened his first bookshop in Camberwell Grove in 1981 and stayed there nine years, finally moving to York when he and his wife decided that they did not want to bring up children in London. He specializes in literature and first editions, but says:

This page: Part of the frontage of Ken Spelman's shop in Micklegate, York.
Opposite: As seen *circa* 1910, the site in Micklegate, York, now occupied by Ken Spelman's shop.

79
EDWIN STORY
OOKSELLERS STATIONERS

"It takes a long time to get to know your customers in York: they drift in and out like flotsam and jetsam and never ask advice. I could be selling ice cream. The customers who know what they're doing tend to go to Ken Spelman. If they have time they come down Fossgate, but I'm only one of several bookshops they might visit.

"At some stage I will probably have to learn about the internet. Although I find it good for reference, I much prefer to look for books in a bookshop. Almost anybody's stock is an education. It amazes me how people come into a shop, barely stop, and walk out again – even people in the trade. If a stock is any good at all, it's worth investigating, slowly."

Inspired by Rupert Hart-Davis, Mr Ramsden has published books through Stone Trough, with the printing and binding done by Smith Settle of Otley. "We did a little book together of Rupert's tributes to writers, called *Praise From the Past* – people like T. S. Eliot, Siegfried Sassoon, Arthur Ransome, Neville Cardus. Rupert didn't have great visual sophistication, but he was an incredibly good proof reader, even in his late eighties. He regarded mistakes in the text as almost morally wrong."

Ken Spelman in Micklegate, established over half a century, has the prosperous feel that goes with a varied, well-displayed stock and unobtrusively busy staff. The day I was there I happened to cross the road afterwards and found a book sale, mainly of religious works, going on in a derelict church. There was a sad and dusty air about it all, but it still reminded me of a rather different case – Charles Leakey's Inverness bookshop, which is housed in a converted church, with the sales desk at the base of the pulpit, and treats its customers to superior music, not too loud. During one visit I was able to hear a complete performance of Beethoven's ninth symphony.

Kim's, Worthing

I have been going to Worthing every year since 1981, reporting from the various bowls championships at Beach House Park and, in spare moments – of which there are many in a slow sport such as bowls

– browsing to and fro in the town's second-hand bookshops. The first of these that I got to know was the Steyne, at the junction of the High Street and the Brighton road, five minutes' walk from the site of the house where Oscar Wilde wrote *The Importance of Being Earnest*; but the last time I passed the shop it was boarded up. It had been there twenty years, with a plentiful stock spread over three floors.

Farther west, in Gratwicke Road, is Badgers, which is almost the same age as the Steyne but apparently prospering in much more cramped quarters. I was introduced to Badgers by a journalist-friend of mine, Patrick Sullivan, who usually stayed in Gratwicke Road, in a guest-house owned by Rupert Webb, the old Sussex wicketkeeper. Patrick would saunter along in the late morning to the little press room in Beach House Park and tell me, as a fellow-collector, of any bowls books he has seen in Badgers and which he thought might interest me. Sometimes they did, but not nearly so often as would have been the case with other sports, because it has to be said, with sadness and disappointment, that the general books about bowls are far outnumbered by the instructional ones, which all, in their solemn if different ways, say the same things. There is more to any game than technical minutiae.

One of the best discoveries I have made at Badgers was nothing to do with bowls – two shelves of W. H. Hudson and Richard Jefferies; and over a longish period I picked up, to give only titles that come immediately to mind, Hudson's *Far Away and Long Ago* and *Afoot in England*, as well as Morley Roberts's semi-biographical book about him. Hudson and Jefferies are buried in Broadwater cemetery in Worthing.

Almost backing on to Badgers is Kim's, in Crescent Road, which runs parallel with Gratwicke Road, just off the seafront. It has had four homes in its time, all in Crescent Road, and is now at number nineteen. It was opened in 1971 by Kim Francombe, after she had gained useful experience in antiques markets and postal bookselling, and after a dealer friend, impressed by the number of books in the Francombe household, had suggested they take a stall in a local market. Trade flourished and Kim's bookshop came into being.

Mrs Francombe's daughter, Lin Flowers, joined the business

straight from school, and now Mrs Flowers's daughter helps out too, making it a real family concern, with a relaxed approach much appreciated by the customers. Their shop stretches a long way back, in an inviting perspective of books, with the subject categories clearly indicated by overhead cards and the bulk of the stock in alphabetical order according to authors' names. (I emphasize this point yet again because by no means all shops take the necessary trouble). There are no specialities apart from the sheet music, which is housed separately at the back, next to a room containing books on music, the cinema, theology, and so on. In an outside passageway are the "honesty boxes" – the bargains for anybody with twenty-five pence to spend.

Kim's initial stock in 1971 was a thousand. Now it is close on fifty thousand, and Mrs Flowers says they will send a van to collect from anywhere in England. I asked her the highest price paid by a single customer and she replied: "Five thousand pounds. It was for an elephant folio, a sort of monster coffee-table book, called *The Holy Land*, by David Roberts."

Hall's, Tunbridge Wells

Hall's is one of the oldest second-hand bookshops in the country. It was first opened for business in 1898, in Chapel Place, a short thoroughfare between the Pantiles and the High Street, behind the Church of King Charles the Martyr, which has associations with Samuel Pepys and John Evelyn.

Reuben Hall, described by Harry Pratley, a subsequent owner of Hall's, as "a rather dour Nonconformist, with somewhat restricted views of life," was the founder. Formerly a clerk in a Maidstone brewery, he had only an amateur's knowledge of books, and was no great reader, but he did enjoy dealing in books, and ran Hall's until handing it over to Charles Avery in 1922.

Ten years later Avery sold the shop to Pratley, a Pickwickian figure and one of the best-known booksellers of his generation; and it was during his ownership that, just before the second world war, Hall's moved a few yards along to its present home on a corner, at numbers

Hall's in Tunbridge Wells, which was saved from closure in 1988 by a public outcry.

twenty and twenty-two Chapel Place. Elizabeth Bateman succeeded Pratley as proprietor in 1967 and Sabrina Izzard took over in 1983. She is still there, still determined to preserve the shop's original character and to avoid indiscriminate change. "About the only thing I did when I became the owner," she said, "was to put in new lighting."

In 1988 she and the shop survived a crisis. The adjacent bank which owns the site declined to renew the lease because it wanted to extend its own premises. There was a public outcry, at first local, then national, and finally international. Authors, academics and senior politicians, including Denis Healey and Antonia Fraser, wrote to the broadsheet press, and local people transferred their bank accounts elsewhere. In the end the bank leasing the site took a more enlightened view and relented. Hall's was saved.

Furnished in warm old woodwork, it has a basement and two floors, and a stock of some twenty thousand volumes catering for most tastes; but it does not specialize. I am not a collector in the sense of being systematic or of regarding books as so many trophies of the chase. I prefer to pick up a book here, and a book there, on spec, often something unusual. At Hall's I bought Robert Hichens's 1894 novel *The Green Carnation*, a satire on the Aesthetic movement, its main characters being based on Oscar Wilde and Lord Alfred Douglas; I have a weakness for amusing stories about men – and women – about town in London society. I also noticed on the shelves a copy of that wonderful Guernsey novel, *The Book of Ebenezer Le Page*, by G. B. (Gerald) Edwards – and wondered how any sensitive bibliophile could bear to part with it.

Harry Pratley served Hall's from 1919 until 1967, first as an apprentice at seven shillings a week, and then as owner for thirty-five years. He died in 1987. In 1990 his tape-recorded reminiscences were published by the Hurtwood Press in a little book, *A Bookseller Remembers*, and Richard Goffin, an old friend of the shop, wrote in the introduction:

"Everything [in the shop] remains largely unchanged and the atmosphere is essentially Pratley, so that visitors from all over the world still feel the same welcome continuity and the presence of Harry's benevolent spirit.

"His gusto for books never slackened, to the end of his life he took an almost physical pleasure from a fine binding or rare text."

Arundel

"Can you tell me the way to the High Street?" I asked the ticket clerk on my arrival at Arundel station, and she said, pointing: "Straight down the main road. Head for the castle. Twelve minutes."

If you happen to know what to look for, you can spot the Arundel Bookshop even before you come to the bridge over the river. It is on the other side, at the near end of the High Street, number ten, and has a red awning over the pavement. Towering above it, behind the roofs to the right, is the castle.

"I know of no town with so low a pulse as this precipitous little settlement," E. V. Lucas wrote in his book on Sussex. "In spite of the picnic parties in the park, in spite of anglers from London, in spite of the railway in the valley, Arundel is still medieval and curiously foreign. On a very hot day, as one climbs the hill to the cathedral, one might be in old France, and certainly in the Middle Ages."

He would have hesitated to write of a low pulse now. Arundel has become a magnet for visitors by the coachload. The Saturday I was there, towards the end of April, I saw no coaches – it was too early in the year even for them; but I heard American and Asian accents, and it was plain that the advance guard of the annual invasion force of tourists had arrived.

The bookshop is well positioned in the town to attract passing trade. Previously a gift shop, it was started in a small way in 1977 by Guy Shepherd and his wife Ann, and they have built up the stock to between twelve and fifteen thousand – not a huge number as these things go, but good for browsers with catholic tastes, Mrs Shepherd says, and everything from astrology to world wars on offer. I noted a strong collection of Georges Simenon and Maigret. Mr Shepherd used to work in antiques and technical journalism, but he and his wife had always wanted to own a second-hand bookshop, and saw the need for one in Arundel. They are now open seven days a week.

The Arundel Bookshop, started by a husband and wife to fulfil a shared ambition.

Even going from one shop to the next for the purposes of this book, I did not reckon to make a purchase on every visit. Nevertheless, I came away from Arundel with *Souvenirs*, Roy Fuller's memoir of his childhood and youth in Lancashire. Fuller, it will be remembered, led a professional double life, combining a career as novelist and poet with another as legal adviser to the Woolwich Building Society. I have read two of the novels, *Image of a Society* and *The Ruined Boys*, and feel drawn to Fuller's reticent, Anthony Powell-esque style and manifest love of music. But his books are hard to find now, when reticence is seen in some quarters as a weakness.

My edition of *Souvenirs*, which has a sepia photograph of Blackpool beach on the cover, was published by the *London Magazine* in 1980 – a reminder of the late Alan Ross's indefatigable work not only for the magazine that he edited for so long, but also on behalf of many new or unfashionable writers. The few writers I have met, mostly through newspapers, were not just unfashionable but unknown. There was one occasion, however, when I did nearly meet a famous writer. When I worked on the sports desk of *The Times* in Gray's Inn Road, some of the sub-editors would adjourn to a certain pub for their supper break. One evening they came back and told me they had been talking to Laurie Lee.

Staffs, Lichfield

Before starting work on this book I advertised for information and received a letter from Mrs Susan Rear telling me of "an excellent second-hand bookshop here in Lichfield – the Staffs Bookshop, now owned by Peter Stockham. He used to have a shop in Cecil Court, off Charing Cross Road, but returned to his home city in 1989, buying from Hazel Morton, who was running the shop for her uncle. Mr Morton had had the shop in the old part of the city, on Dam Street, the street leading up to the south-east gate of the cathedral close, since 1936.

"I worked for Hazel for about three years and then for Peter, part-time, in this delightful shop on two floors. Mr Morton had sold school texts through the years and had many old customers who kept in contact. I still correspond with a just-retired professor of linguistics at Regensburg University."

The Staffs building dates from the fourteenth century and Mr Stockham's wife, Anne, said it was a private house before it became a bookshop in the 1930s. In Sheppard's directory of book dealers the shop invites you to "visit our Aladdin's cave, with more than thirty thousand second-hand, antiquarian and select new books." Specialities, with appropriate catalogues, include children's books, dolls, fine printing, literature and of course Samuel Johnson, who was born in Lichfield and began his formal schooling in Dam Street, at a dame school run by a confectioner called Ann Oliver.

Lichfield deserves a bookshop as good as the Staffs, and not only because of Johnson. It has a variety of literary connections, with the playwright George Farquhar, the essayist Joseph Addison, the actor David Garrick, and the scientist and poet Erasmus Darwin, grandfather of Charles. Johnson's father sold books, and Lichfield's public library was only the second in England when it was established in the nineteenth century.

The bookshop closed early the day I visited Lichfield and so I had less time than I would have liked to browse. But it was long enough to get a sense of the place and of the continual to-ing and fro-ing of keen customers around the dozen or so rooms.

I read Proust in the 1970s – it took me eight years to complete the course – and the Staffs had a copy of *By Way of Sainte-Beuve*, the miscellaneous writings of Proust. In its portraits of painters section there is an unfinished essay on Chardin, the best of its kind I have read, advising "a young man of limited means and artistic tastes" how to look at pictures and penetrate beyond the canvas to their meanings. I am no lover of art galleries, with their airlessness and *poseur* element, but mindful of Proust's essay I went to the Chardin exhibition at the Royal Academy and thought how much more illuminating the catalogue would have been if it had contained at least some of what Proust wrote on the subject.

My father served throughout the first world war and one of his favourite books was Ian Hay's *The First Hundred Thousand*, about a

Scottish infantry regiment. I did not know there was a sequel, *Carrying On*, but there it was on the Staffs shelves, along with some of Hay's other novels. Who reads Ian Hay now? Who has heard of him, even? I think his full name was Ian Hay Beith.

Mrs Rear ended her letter to me with a recommendation for another second-hand bookshop, three miles away at Burntwood: Sheppard's gives its address as Farewell Lane and its proprietors as Kenneth Hayward and Royden Smith. It is open only at weekends and, Mrs Rear says, is "very cheap and full of bargain treasures."

Baggins, Rochester

Baggins Book Bazaar, to give it its full title, claims to be the largest second-hand bookshop in England, and after traversing its premises at the Medway end of Rochester High Street, round the corner from the cathedral, you would not care to dispute the fact. Half a million books are housed in a building that used to be motor-cycle showrooms; they stretch from front to rear, in a narrow switchback of stairs and landings, culminating in windows that you can see from the train.

Rochester being in Charles Dickens country, it would have been all too easy to steal a name for the shop from his novels. Instead, they settled on Bilbo Baggins, the hobbit in J. R. Tolkien, and the shop was opened in 1986 by a former London bookseller, Paul Minet. A few doors along is Baggins Too, much more recently opened, and dealing in non-fiction overflow from the parent store. Upstairs in the bazaar is a room where local artists can exhibit their work; but this space may eventually be gobbled up by yet more books.

Godfrey George has been Baggins's manager from the outset. "Rochester may be the 'book city' of the south-east of England," he says. "Besides our two Baggins shops, there are three other general bookshops and a military specialist shop, all within half a mile.

"Baggins is one of the oldest established businesses in the High Street. In a comparatively short time we've seen other shops come and go, we've battled through the recession of the 'nineties, and we've survived a few years of difficult trading in general in Rochester. And

I don't think the fear that internet sales would damage 'proper' bookshops, with everybody buying online, has materialized."

Baggins, which is open seven days a week, does not specialise. It tries to give its customers, some of them coming from as far as Australia, the widest choice possible, without consciously seeking rarities or charging inflated prices. Whatever bookshop I happen to find myself in, I never fail to gravitate sooner or later to the sports shelves, and in Baggins I saw, as I so often do in second-hand shops, Edmund Blunden's *Cricket Country*, which was regarded by Rupert Hart-Davis as one of the two best books ever written about the game, the other being Neville Cardus's *Good Days*. Perhaps Blunden wrote a little too much above the heads of ordinary cricketing readers for his book to be still in demand over half a century after it was written. Hence its fate to lie now among the frequently unwanted.

Mention of Cardus reminds me that his *A Cricketer's Book*, first published by Grant Richards in 1922, with an introduction by Cardus's boyhood hero, A. C. MacLaren, is one of only two first editions I possess (the other is Bernard Darwin's *The English Public School*). I paid, I think, forty pounds for it to Martin Wood, who has been selling cricket books and publications of all kinds from private premises in Sevenoaks since 1970, first in St John's Road, and now at 1c Wickenden Road. He estimates his stock of real books, as opposed to county annuals, programmes, cards, etc, at three thousand – a remarkable total for a single subject. But then, cricket *is* singular.

Camden, Bath

I first visited Bath in the early 1960s. I went for the festival, whose presiding genius in those days was Yehudi Menuhin, and stayed in a guest-house called Snow White, each bedroom being named after one of the dwarfs; I slept in Grumpy. Since then I have been back to Bath fairly regularly, for this reason or that, usually journalistic and connected with rugby; but here I am sampling the city's second-hand bookshops.

You encounter the first of them, and certainly the largest, as soon as you walk out of the railway station. This is Bayntun's, in a grand old building, a converted postal sorting-office, at the head of Manvers Street. George Bayntun founded his own bookbinding business in Bath in 1894 and branched out into bookselling with the purchase of George Gregory's extensive stock in Green Street in 1920; Gregory's goes back even further than Bayntun's, to 1845.

After Bayntun's death at the beginning of the second world war (by which time he had been appointed Bookseller to Her Majesty Queen Mary), Gregory's was sold and business declined, not reviving until 1954 when the founder's grandson, Hylton Bayntun-Coward, took over. Ownership of Gregory's was regained, prosperity slowly returned, and Bayntun's shop and showroom now combine a healthy second-hand and antiquarian trade with specialization in fine new and old bindings.

From Manvers Street I crossed Pulteney bridge, turned left, and found Walcot Street, which has a bohemian air about it as it winds on, past a variety of quaint little shops, to St Swithin's church, where Jane Austen's parents were married and her father is buried. Opposite the church is the Camden bookshop.

At one time used by the Natural Theatre Company, organizers of street entertainments, and before that as a hairdresser's, the shop was a ruin when it came into the hands of Victor Suchar and his wife Elizabeth in 1984. It took the best part of a year to get straight, and now every available inch is covered in books, with a scholarly bias reflected in the stock of subjects such as classical antiquity, economic theory, mathematics, and physics. These are to be found mainly in Mr Suchar's eyrie on the upper floor, which is not open to the public, while Mrs Suchar sits downstairs among the slightly less forbidding shelves of literature, biography and the like.

"Five million books are published in the world every year," Mr Suchar says. "Only one per cent of them are any good, and settle, and they end up in second-hand shops."

Mr Suchar was born in Switzerland but has American citizenship, having lived eighteen years in New York when he worked as a structural engineer. His wife is American, born in Virginia, and was a teacher in London before they moved to Bath. They can be discerned in the painting of the interior of the shop, done by a local artist, Richard Lannoy, in what he terms his Cézanne style. It hangs by the staircase and I would say captures the atmosphere not just of Camden Books but of all the most likable of these bookshops.

It is instructive to hear customers' requests, and while I was browsing a woman came in to ask for books on Loch Ness without the monster, and a man wanted the work of certain American novelists. And when I was discussing with Mr Suchar the book you are reading now, another customer, overhearing us, asked me: "Ever been to New York? Do you know the Strand bookstore on Broadway? It's the best anywhere, and it's twice the size of Waterstone's." I made a note.

I saw in the Camden an elegant copy of Giuseppe di Lampedusa's *The Leopard*, a memorable novel (one of the few I have read twice), made into almost as memorable a film; and a first edition of *The Funny Bone*, comprising shorter pieces by Julian Maclaren-Ross, one of Soho's bohemians in the 1940s and later. (I have heard one of Maclaren-Ross's short stories, "I had to go sick", read by Harold Pinter on radio). I also saw, adjacent to *The Funny Bone*, what I hastily believed to be a first edition of *Animal Farm*, but it turned out to be a second.

Petersfield

The Petersfield Bookshop was founded in 1918 by Harry Roberts, an East End of London doctor who helped to start the panel scheme that preceded the National Health Service. Finding no bookshop when he moved to Petersfield, he decided to open one of his own, at the suggestion of a local artist, Flora Twort. A Miss Brahms looked after the books, Miss Twort had her studio there, and a Miss Wagstaffe made jewellery, illustrated books and produced prints.

That shop was in The Square, but the business was bought in 1958 by Frank Westwood, who moved it to its present home in Chapel Street, where he and his wife Ann, and their sons David and John, work in partnership. The premises next door, once a slaughterhouse, were purchased in 1973, enabling the stock to be considerably enlarged, and there is an annexe in Station Road. The price range is between fifty pence and two thousand pounds.

Entering through a pillared forecourt full of paperbacks, you arrive at a maze of shelves with directions to just about every subject you might reasonably expect to find. I was impressed by the children's section and its old *Boy's Own Paper* and *Girl's Own Paper* annuals. In the *BOP* there were stories by Charles Gilson, my favourite author of boys' books; he is mentioned in approving terms in Graham Greene's essay "The Lost Childhood," so my boy's instinct all those years ago, during the second world war, must have been sound. Gilson had military rank, varying from captain to major, as did F. S. Brereton, who might be promoted, between books, from captain to lieutenant-colonel. I have often speculated on the careers of such men, and how they came to make a living in the way they did, but all my research has been unproductive. There seems to be no source of biographical detail concerning the more obscure writers for children. I also saw in Petersfield *Young England* annuals, twenty or so Enid Blyton stories, some Henty and Billy Bunter, but no Just William, another of my boyhood addictions.

First editions old and modern had their own glass-fronted cabinets, and there were sets of English literature in marbled bindings, including one of Sir Walter Scott from the middle of the nineteenth century. P. G. Wodehouse was well represented among the moderns, and an unusual item was a row of bound issues of the literary magazine *Horizon*, which was founded and edited by Cyril Connolly.

Promising collections of books are visited anywhere by the Westwoods, with angling, exploration, transport and colonial history among the specialities. Valuations for insurance are undertaken, and there is a book-binding and repair service. The shop has appointments to the Queen as picture framer and supplier of artists' materials and to the Prince of Wales as picture framer. Mrs Westwood's particular enthusiasm is rare dolls and she has specimens from her collection on display.

Afterwards we adjourned to the Old Stables restaurant and tea-rooms for lunch, noting that it had won the gold award in its class in the Petersfield in Bloom competition of 2000. We thought it deserved another gold award for its food – and, not least, for the fact that it inflicts no background music whatever on its customers. We then walked round Heath Pond, which looks about three times the size of the Round Pond in Kensington Gardens, and returned to the Old Stables for afternoon tea, after which it was time to go home.

Howes, Hastings

A correspondent, James Lancaster, wrote to me from France saying that Howes is his favourite antiquarian bookshop and praising its "remarkable stock, knowledgeable staff and erudite catalogues." You do not have to be there long to see what he means.

The shop is a redbrick building in Braybrooke Terrace, five minutes on foot from the railway station, and at one time was the parish school of Holy Trinity. Charles Howes, who served his apprenticeship in Oxford, first opened for business in 1921, in small premises near the public library in the town centre of Hastings. He left to work as an itinerant actor and stage manager but returned quite soon to bookselling, and after the war his firm, having by then settled in Braybrooke Terrace, went from strength to strength.

Its catalogues are displayed on a table in the entrance hall; when I visited, they included one for the historical portion of A. L. Rowse's library and another for Latin and Greek classics once owned by Enoch Powell. You then pass through into two rooms – more accurately described as halls, on account of their size – which at first have the feeling of a library rather than a bookshop; everything is hushed and orderly. There are no "Quiet, please" notices, but you could imagine their presence.

A mile of purpose-built shelving holds a massive antiquarian and second-hand stock, strong on the humanities, literature and church history; and there is a section clearly marked for first editions, although Miles Bartley, Howes' managing director, told me that they do not specialize in these, among which I noted Barrie, Wells, Priestley and Dylan Thomas. I also saw Otto Jahn's famous biography of Mozart, in German, and published in Leipzig in 1856. I have never come across an English translation, but presumably there must be such a thing.

Hastings these days has a run-down, even slum appearance in parts, and you have to seek out the narrow, hilly side streets for the best of the town's character. It was while we were doing this that we saw a plaque on a house in Exmouth Place recording the fact that Catherine Cookson had lived there in the early 1930s.

Farther down towards East Cliff, in the Old Town, we investigated the High Street Bookshop, which was as great a contrast to Howes as could be imagined. Hardbacks rubbed against paperbacks, and there were fluffy animal toys hanging up, all with captions, one of which I copied out: "Hello. I'm a polar bear. I sit next to the travel books. Ask the rabbit for countryside books."

At the last moment I picked out and bought *Son of London*, by Thomas Burke, dedicated "To a London suburb, with the author's love." He does not name the suburb but from hints he drops I think it might be Camberwell. The shop's owner casually remarked that Burke was the man who wrote *Limehouse Nights*, a book of near-the-knuckle short stories ("ugly but not obscene" was one contemporary verdict) admired by Bernard Shaw and Arnold Bennett and published, apparently at considerable legal risk, by Grant Richards during the first world war. It was a great success, here and in America. Richards, a flamboyant, monocled figure, with a gambler's instinct, published Neville Cardus's first book, and Cardus mentions *Limehouse Nights* in his autobiography. Otherwise the title would have meant nothing to me, and I might never have bought *Son of London*. Burke wrote a number of books about England in general and London in particular, and was a novelist too.

Steedman, Newcastle

Before going north again, I paid a visit to the antiquarian book fair at Olympia, where the exhibitors ranged, alphabetically, from Theodor Ackermann of Munich to Graham York Rare Books of Honiton. I am one of those people, surely the overwhelming majority, who look on books, first, last and all the time, as reading-matter, not as fantastically expensive objects, however rare, to be tracked down and kept in locked cabinets. I prefer books to be well designed and printed, but for me appearance is always secondary to content. Nevertheless, as I had not been to such an event before, the fair was an interesting experience. I noted the following exhibits as typical:

> An uncorrected proof copy of J. K. Rowling's *Harry Potter and the Philosopher's Stone* – £5,000;
> Rider Haggard's copy of Gibbon's *The Decline and Fall of the Roman Empire* – £1,500;
> Virginia Woolf's pocket engagement diaries – £70,000;
> A first edition of James Joyce's *Ulysses* (Shakespeare and Company, Paris) – £23,500.

There are two second-hand bookshops in Newcastle, one belonging to David Steedman, who had a stand at Olympia. His grandfather, Robert Steedman, founded the Grey Street firm in 1907; the present Mr Steedman took over in the 1960s and runs it now with one assistant, David Entwistle, where once he had five.

Their stock, though not large, is attractive, with all the predictable sets of Shakespeare, Dickens, Scott and Thackeray, but also of men like Montaigne. Local history is a strong feature, with a good selection of books by or about Thomas Bewick, the eighteenth-century Tyneside wood engraver; and I saw a handsome four-volume 1915 first edition of Archibald Thorburn's *British Birds*, inclusive of the supplement and priced at £1,200.

William Macneile Dixon's *The Human Situation* caught my eye, too. It comprises his Gifford lectures in philosophy, delivered at Glasgow University during 1935–37, and since reprinted many times. My copy, much stained, was bought at a church book sale in Muswell Hill thirty years ago, when I was discovering the work of Schopenhauer, Oswald Spengler and Bertrand Russell. I was deeply impressed by Macneile Dixon's humane and all-embracing approach to a subject too often reduced to abstractions; it is an approach he makes clear in the course of his introduction:

"Not a few men have at times breathed the wish that God or nature had upon the great fundamental problems of life broken the spell of silence. Yet, perhaps, we should not desire it, since it may well be for the benefit of both mind and soul that it remains unbroken . . .

"There are in the realm of thought no absolute authorities, no dictators. No man, living or dead, can claim oracular powers. Mine is a personal view. All philosophies are in the end personal. You can no more escape your philosophy than you can escape your own shadow, for it also is a reflection of yourself. Systems of thought are the shadows cast by different races, epochs and civilisations."

A short walk from Steedman's is the city's other second-hand booksellers – the Newcastle Bookshop ("You never know what you might find"), almost hidden in an alleyway off The Side, at the foot of Dean Street. It is a real higgledy-piggledy mixture, books of many kinds, including first editions of Aldous Huxley, sharing the limited space with long-playing gramophone records and antiquarian prints. Upstairs is a photographic gallery where the theme, the day I saw it, was the foot-and-mouth epidemic of the time. Should you thirst for a cappuccino, there is a bistro close at hand.

I spent a total of three hours in these two shops. On the return journey to London my train was halted for nearly as long by what was officially described over the public address system as "a lightning strike" in the Darlington area. To me the phrase "lightning strike" instantly suggested industrial action, but it turned out to mean signals struck by lightning. Such is the misleadingness of a familiar locution thoughtlessly used.

Tombland, Norwich

The signs on the approach roads to Norwich proclaim A Fine City; and it has fine second-hand bookshops, in themselves a sign of a civilised place. The Tombland is in a street of that name, on two floors, opposite the cathedral and next door to a public-house called the Edith Cavell. John Freeman and his wife, Alison, have been running it for a dozen years and more, after a similar period in Cardiff, and they have a branch, known as Freeman's Corner, not far away on King Street, which Mr Freeman emphasised is not an overflow shop but one with the same wide range of stock as the Tombland.

Routinely, I asked how many books he thought he had on his shelves, and he said several thousands, adding with a certain pride: "What you see in our two shops is only the tip of the iceberg. We've got books lying around everywhere, in barns, stables, garages, attics. There are probably half a million in all."

Drif's name came up in conversation, as it tended to do during these visits, and Mr Freeman turned out to be an admirer of that nonconformist guide to second-hand bookshops. "You have to take Drif as you find him," he said. "He loathes serried rows of academic books, pretentiousness, book fairs, and things like that, and I share his prejudices. Drif is passionate about second-hand books and isn't afraid to show it. He even had a kind word for us."

I am neither a cook nor a gourmet, and the only book I have read on cookery is Elizabeth David's *An Omelette and a Glass of Wine*, which is not confined to the kitchen, being a collection of her journalism, not a string of recipes. The Tombland stocked Lisa Chaney's biography of Mrs David. It also had *Heroes, Mavericks and Bounders: The English Gentleman from Lord Curzon to James Bond*, another social survey by Hugh David, akin to his work on literary Soho, *The Fitzrovians*.

A. J. Cruse's *Cigarette Card Cavalcade*, published in 1948, sent my mind back to my boyhood about that time, when I was an avid collector of regimental uniforms, cricketers, trains and the like, carefully inserting the cards in exercise books and doing "swaps" with other boys – a set of dogs, perhaps, for a set of ships. Many years later, putting sentiment aside and realising that I would never covet another cigarette card, I took my entire collection to a shop in Cecil Court, Charing Cross Road, where they fetched £25.

As I was leaving, Mr Freeman's dog, a Lakeland terrier cross, appeared and lay down on some books beneath the reception desk. I bought *Writing in a War*, an anthology of prose and poetry of the second world war, edited by Ronald Blythe; took tea in the cathedral refectory; and, just as the evening rush-hour was revving up, walked down King Street to Freeman's Corner, which is on one floor and has a healthy stock of fiction, children's and adult. There was a row of Dornford Yates and almost as many by a writer as different from Yates as could be – Henry Miller, including his *Tropic of Cancer,* once described by Colin MacInnes as "a great prophetic book", praised in chorus by many others, but seen in a dismissive light now – a common fate of contemporary criticism.

My wife, meanwhile, had discovered the Dormouse bookshop, on Elm Hill, five minutes' walk from the Tombland. There I spotted W. H. Hudson's *Idle Days in Patagonia* (an odd place to be idle in, as Edward Thomas observed), but it was a spoiled copy, with the title on the spine obliterated by usage, and I decided to wait for a better.

Gibb's, Manchester

In the city of the Hallé and the BBC Philharmonic and the Lindsay quartet, Gibb's has one of the best selections of books on music, as well as of recorded music, that I have seen, leaving aside specialist shops such as the late Charles Macdonald's at Steyning in Sussex. The Bridgewater Hall, home of the Hallé, is within walking distance of Gibb's in Lower Mosley Street, and so is the College of Music in Oxford Road.

Gibb's Bookshop Ltd is now in Charlotte Street, a turning off to the left as you go down Mosley Street from Piccadilly. It was originally opened in Liverpool by Robert Gibb in 1922, moving to Manchester thirteen years later, and it is still a family business, the present proprietors being the founder's son, Anthony, his wife, Anne, and their son, Robert.

It is a shop with no specialities, and no fiction either, apart from classics in Everyman editions – this for reasons of space, the previous premises in Mosley Street, which included a warehouse, having been more roomy. There is much by or about Manchester and Mancunians in stock, including rarely-seen books by Allan Monkhouse, a playwright and dramatic critic during C. P. Scott's editorship of the *Manchester Guardian*; he was described by Neville Cardus as "an artist in shades so fine that compared to him Henry James was substantial, not to say carnal."

An uncle of mine was a West End doctor in private practice for half a century. He belonged to the same London club – the Arts in Dover Street, I think – as Sir Alfred Munnings, about whom he often employed a four-letter noun – an opinion that seems to have been pretty general. I recalled this on seeing Munnings's autobiography, *An Artist's Life*, on Gibb's shelves.

Turning to the music section, I noted copies of Bernard Shore's two books. Shore played the viola in the BBC Symphony Orchestra between the wars, under some of the greatest conductors, among them Toscanini, and he wrote of these experiences in *The Orchestra Speaks* – an ironic title, given that orchestras rarely have the opportunity to speak at all when self-important conductors (who are usually the worst conductors) are on the podium. Of Toscanini, however, Shore did not have a bad word to say. He followed *The Orchestra Speaks* with *Sixteen Symphonies*, an executant's view of symphonies and their composers from Haydn to Walton. His accounts make refreshing reading after the dense technicalities of most programme-note writers.

Musical Chairs, the highly opinionated autobiography of Cecil Gray, another *Manchester Guardian* critic, was there, as were Marion Scott's lovingly-written life of Beethoven and Alfred Einstein's *Schubert*. Dame Ethel Smyth described Schubert's music as "that crystal stream welling and welling for ever"; after listening to a Schubert chamber work, Kenneth Tynan wrote in his diary that "there is nothing more beautiful than the happy moments of unhappy men"; and, more recently, Simon Jenkins suggested in *The Times* that a whole radio wavelength could be devoted to Schubert, so prodigious were his output and gifts of melody and invention.

The classical recording industry is dying, according to columnists like Norman Lebrecht, but you would find that hard to believe as you look along the racks of records and compact discs in shops like Gibb's. Long-playing records of concertos and boxed sets of operas were going at fifty pence each when I visited, and there were off-the-beaten-track things – the complete Bruckner symphonies conducted by Georg Tintner, and performances by pianists from the past such as Alfred

Brendel's teacher, Edwin Fischer – to stimulate the collector. I too used to be a collector, buying my first LP in 1955, and when I came to London in 1960, and was unhappy working for the *Daily Telegraph*, I applied for a post on *The Gramophone*, journeying out hopefully to that magazine's address in Stanmore; but nothing came of my efforts.

Fifteenth Century, Lewes

Few bookshops appear on local postcards, but the Fifteenth Century, at ninety-nine Lewes High Street, does. It is the second oldest building in Lewes, the castle being the oldest, and the first house to have been built outside the town walls. The shop's name gives you some idea when it was built, but nobody knows exactly, although the Sussex Archaeological Society places it about 1450.

Records of previous occupants go no further back than the middle of the eighteenth century, when clay-pipe makers carried on business there. It was a subscription library, and then a confectioner's, before becoming a bookshop in 1936. Eric Blundell, a Bloomsbury bookseller before the second world war, took over eventually, and the present proprietor is Susan Mirabaud.

You can scarcely see her for books as you enter the half-timbered shop, stooping to do so. The roof is low and the piled-up stock has to be negotiated with care. Much of it in the front part is for children – stories by Elinor Brent Dyer, W. E. Johns, Frank Richards, Malcolm Saville, Richmal Crompton, Enid Blyton and Elsie Oxenham, among others. And to emphasise this bias towards children, there are teddy bears for sale.

I remember the Wonder Book series from my boyhood. One of my favourites was the *Wonder Book of Daring Deeds*, a topical title as I was on the verge of my 'teens during the war. It was as pleasing to see several Wonder books in the Fifteenth Century as it was to see old *Chums* annuals, with their tales of adventure by Gunby Hadath, Charles Gilson and D. H. Parry, and colour plates (what an evocative word is "plates"!) by Stanley Wood, which I would try to copy in pencil and crayon.

Lewes is uncommonly well off for second-hand bookshops, with at least five in the High Street alone. The Bow Windows, established in 1964 and owned by Alan and Jennifer Shelley, used to be at 128, a former public-house, but moved to 175 six years ago. It specialises in the endless saga of the Bloomsbury group; and I saw first editions of four novels by another celebrated, if half forgotten Victorian, Marie Corelli, dated 1896 and with revealing titles like *Temporal Power* and *The Life Everlasting.*

Cumming's is near the Bow Windows, on the opposite side of the street, and has a fine stock of English and European literature. There was a complete set of Hazlitt, twenty-one volumes – I had not realised he wrote so much; what could have been a complete W. H. Hudson; and a suitably long shelf of Balzac. Edgar Wallace may have been in his own line as copious as Balzac, and many of his novels were on tempting display in their uniform red covers in Cumming's windows.

My last call in Lewes was on Caburn Books, up the hill from the railway station. It was notable, to me, for its request to customers not to use their mobile phones while in the shop. I am a member of the long-suffering minority who do not regard a mobile as essential, one of my reasons being that, far from wanting to remain in constant touch with the human race, for business, pleasure or anything else, I am often delighted to feel completely cut off from it.

I bought in Caburn's an Everyman edition of Mary Russell Mitford's *Our Village*, one of the countless books I have long been intending to read. Miss Mitford died in 1855, having spent almost her entire life in county towns and villages on the borderland of Hampshire and Berkshire – "not very far," J. C. Squire wrote in his introduction, "from the haunts of Jane Austen and White of Selborne, neither of whom was a more exact observer than she or acquainted with as wide a range of rural life. . . . She found all she wanted in a few square miles, and knew it. 'Even in books,' she said, 'I like a confined locality.'"

Chapel Books, Westleton

Escaping the worst of a London heatwave, we spent a few days in north Norfolk, staying in Wells-next-the-Sea and returning home through Westleton, a village between Southwold and Aldeburgh in Suffolk. We had remembered Chapel Books from past visits, and it was still there, opposite the post office and backing on to a duck pond.

Its premises are unheated and Bob Jackson, the owner, regrets there is no access for wheelchairs; but he does offer tea and coffee, and that is an unaccustomed little luxury in a second-hand bookshop. The stock is good, but unevenly distributed, with a tight squeeze among the shelves necessitating frequent muttered apologies between passing customers. Books share the floor space with long-playing records.

The building was last used as a chapel in the 1960s and has been a bookshop since 1982, when Mr Jackson's mother bought it for him: he was on the dole at the time. Before that he had dabbled in teaching, writing and painting, and lived on occasion as a recluse. Taking on the shop was something of a calculated risk, but it is now open seven days a week.

We roamed the countryside from our Wells base and were drawn to Simon Gough's shop on Fish Hill, in Holt. Mr Gough sold it to Tristram Hull some years ago but it still trades under the name Simon Gough. It houses nearly twenty thousand volumes in ten rooms, and I noted among the unexpected items a history of the Shelbourne Hotel in Dublin by the novelist Elizabeth Bowen. Also in Holt there is Jackdaw Books, run by Mick and Eleanor Finn on New Street. They opened for business in 1997. "Both of us had other careers before that," Mrs Finn said, "but we had always wanted to own a second-hand bookshop, and here we are."

As we were leaving, we saw on the counter a basket containing paperback copies of a book called *Poppy-Land*, by Clement Scott, who was a theatre critic and journalistic rival of Bernard Shaw in London in the 1890s. Poppy-Land was the name given by Scott to Cromer and its vicinity, and his book, first published in 1886 and long out of print, is a collection of holiday pieces (what he called "papers") written for the *Daily Telegraph*. Christine Stockwell republished it in 1992 and the latest edition appeared in 2000. There is a reliable sixth-sense that tells us whether or not to buy a book of this unfamiliar kind, and in the case of *Poppy-Land* we bought without hesitation.

As I said, we roamed widely in north Norfolk. We sailed to Blakeney Point to view the seal and tern colonies; looked into churches, including All Saints, Burnham Thorpe, where Horatio Nelson's father had been rector; walked miles along Holkham's lovely deserted pebble-free beach; and lunched in the village of Heydon, described by Candida Lycett Green in her *Travels Through An Unwrecked Landscape* as ". . . little known, on the way to nowhere, quiet, unadulterated, and as near to the pastoral idyll as anywhere in England."

On our last evening in Wells-next-the-Sea we dined at the Corner House restaurant where we saw an unusual sight – unusual to me, at any rate: a husband and wife reading books over their meal – books, mark you, not newspapers. Both looked as though they could have been Anglo-Indian. They spoke to each other, certainly, but only with reference to the food. I could not make out the book the man was so engrossed in, but his wife had something by Kipling: I could tell from the blue cover with the elephant's-head symbol in gilt on the front, the Macmillan collected edition. I first read Kipling in my youth – his *Plain Tales From the Hills*, in the same elegant binding. It planted Mrs Hauksbee in my memory.

Albion, Broadstairs

Broadstairs has more connections of interest than most seaside resorts of its size. Edward Heath used to moor his yacht there, and Charles Dickens holidayed and wrote in the town, prompting a small local industry, some of it genuine, much of it bogus. Less well-known is the fact that John Buchan wrote *The Thirty-Nine Steps* near Stone Bay to relieve the boredom of convalescence. I once set out to try to find what may have been the original steps but gave up the search after a man on the esplanade told me they were now crumbling and dangerous on a private estate.

When Peter Hicks, a friend of mine who works for W. H. Smith, heard of this, he wrote to me: "I have been a Buchan fan since I read *The Thirty-Nine Steps* when I was about thirteen, as my father had the four main Richard Hannay stories in a combined volume in our library. I have since read the tale many times and at present have the cassette read by Robert Powell from the public library.

"When I was last in Scotland I drove along the road Hannay took when he left the train in Galloway (Gatehouse of Fleet) on the way to Creetown. I parked by the side of the road and in my imagination waited for him to appear!"

I came to Buchan through *Prester John*, which I believe he wrote in reaction against the dullness, as he saw it, of the boys' books of his time, and I went on to devour the Hannay stories. *Mr Standfast* was my parents' favourite, as the tattered cover testified, and they were always moved by its closing pages, with the quotation from Bunyan. Buchan is usually discussed now, if at all, in class, political, even racial terms, some of which, for all I know, may be justified; but in my innocence I prefer to see him simply as a great storyteller.

The Albion second-hand shop on Albion Street, just above the pier and Viking Bay, stocked *Prester John*, *Julius Caesar* and *The King's Grace* of Buchan's books, but none of the Hannay novels. Established in 1956 and owned by Alan Kemp, it was converted from a chapel and used as a storeroom for the other Albion shop, dealing in new books, farther up the street, until the purchase of a former greengrocer's premises allowed room for expansion to its present capacity.

Upstairs, where the outlines of the old chapel can best be seen, the fiction is more or less in alphabetical order, but for the most part you have to take the whole stock, which is considerable, as you find it. I read a lot of Westerns in my youth and I saw some of the Sudden books of Oliver Strange, bringing back, by association, such names as Zane Grey, Max Brand, Norman Fox, and the Hopalong Cassidy series of Clarence Mulford. The only Western I have read since those early days is Jack Schaefer's *Shane*, but I still love Western films as much as, if not more than, any other genre in the cinema – and I mean the real thing, in the heroic vein of James Stewart and John Wayne, not the dude-ranch travesties of Roy Rogers. As Michael Parkinson has written: "It's a different world nowadays, nearer reality perhaps than the fantasy West of my youth. But it's still beguiling, more now than ever before."

A Common Reader collection of Virginia Woolf's essays had me looking about in vain for a modern critic able, like her, to bring a novelist's imagination and intensity to the task of literary reviewing. I used to copy out, as if for a commonplace book, things I admired, and I offer as illustration this extract from Mrs Woolf on George Gissing:

"Gissing, indeed, never ceased to educate himself. While the Baker Street trains hissed their steam under his window, and the lodger downstairs blew his room out, and the landlady was insolent, and the grocer refused to send the sugar and he had to fetch it himself, and the fog burnt his throat and he caught cold and never spoke to anybody for three weeks, yet he must drive his pen through page after page and vacillate miserably from one domestic disaster to another – while all this went on with a dreary monotony for which he could only blame the weakness of his own character, the columns of the Parthenon, the hills of Rome, rose above the fogs and the fried-fish shops of the Euston Road."

I have referred elsewhere to the *London Magazine* and its late editor, Alan Ross, and during my afternoon in the Albion I found in a pile of back numbers the issue for June 1957, when it was edited by John Lehmann. It contained a piece by Jocelyn Brooke on coming to London to be interviewed for a post with the BBC. Brooke is best-known (which in his case is not very well-known at all, despite the advocacy of Anthony Powell) for his autobiographical *Orchid Trilogy*, which I have read twice, something I rarely do, with great pleasure. Much of it is set in Kent, though around Hythe and Folkestone, not Broadstairs.

Halewood & Sons, Preston

The Halewoods have been running their business in Friargate for five generations since it was established in 1867. This is a record of continuous ownership unique among second-hand booksellers in the north of England; and it would be difficult, to say the least, to find its like anywhere else.

William Halewood, the founder, was born in Liverpool in 1840, into a family with a seafaring background. While still young he was encouraged to become an itinerant evangelist, but in his twenties entered upon his life's work in bookselling, opening his first shop in Adelphi Street, Preston, before moving to Friargate. There are two shops there now, at numbers thirty-seven and sixty-eight, with William's great-grandson, Horace Halewood, who was born above the shop, having overall responsibility as manager, and his sons, David and Michael, doing the day-to-day work.

In the early years the firm had a branch in Australia. William Halewood's son, Harold, emigrated before 1914 and started a shop in Collins Street, Melbourne, a photograph of which hangs in a store-room in Friargate. But Harold was killed in the Great War, having enlisted in the Anzac forces despite being over the military age limit, and his shop went out of existence. In other ways, though, the over-seas links with Lancashire are still strong, and collectors come to Halewood's from all over the world, drawn by its traditions and the exceptional stock.

Travel is a speciality with them, and so is Sherlock Holmes. Conan Doyle and his immortal detective have been a lifelong interest of Michael Halewood and an entire window of his shop is given over to Sherlockiana. In my youth I read everything of Conan Doyle I could lay my hands on, particularly the Brigadier Gerard tales, and I made my first acquaintance with Sherlock Holmes in an old bound volume of *Strand* magazines which had belonged to my paternal grandfather.

I bought two books in Halewood's, one from each shop – *War on the Line* by Bernard Darwin, and *The Square Egg*, by "Saki". Darwin was golf correspondent of *The Times* for nearly half a century, and a delightful essayist. *War on the Line* shows another facet of his versatility, being a history of the Southern Railway during the second world war; it brings the number of first editions in my possession to three (for the others I refer the reader to my account of Baggins' shop in Rochester).

The Square Egg contains some shorter works of H. H. Munro

("Saki") and a biography of him by his sister Ethel. It was news to me that "Saki" had written plays, but there are three here, along with sketches about topics as diverse as bird life on the Western Front (where "Saki" was killed by a sniper's bullet in 1916) and what he saw as the alleged romance of business. "Whenever I feel in the least tempted to be business-like or methodical or even decently industrious," he wrote, "I go to Kensal Green and look at the graves of those who died in business."

Other Men's Flowers, Field Marshal Earl Wavell's anthology of poetry, also caught my eye. At the time I was trying to trace the source of these haunting lines:

> From the lone shieling of the misty island
> Mountains divide us, and the waste of seas –
> Yet still the blood is strong, the heart is Highland,
> And we in dreams behold the Hebrides.

And idly turning the pages I found them in Wavell, who tells us in a footnote: "Attributed to D. M. Moir, but the authorship is disputed. Someone has even troubled to write a whole book on this literary problem." The verse I quote comes, apparently, from a longer poem, "The Canadian Boat Song."

In my youth I went through a poetry-writing phase, as numberless folk do. I attempted various forms, from mannered sonnets and humorous rhymes to an "epic" – that is, far too long – poem with bullfighting for its unlikely subject. I did not persevere sufficiently to find out if I had the true poetic gift, but the discipline of compression and the experience of strange rhythms were more than useful. I sent specimens of my work to John Betjeman and he replied from Wantage that "If you are born to be a poet, no hardship, no lack of recognition will stop you being one. I think you have something in what you write. It is not dull and it is not dead."

I also approached Christopher Fry, who was then living near Brecon, and he wrote back: "Sometimes I feel that you are writing against the inclination of your subject, contorting it by the words rather than expressing it, as though we had caught you, too soon, at the moment of tempering, instead of receiving from you the finished sharp blade."

Back numbers of now-defunct literary magazines have a fascination of their own and Halewood's offered thirty-five issues of *Encounter* (editor, Stephen Spender) from the 1950s for £85. Will back numbers of magazines of our day seem as alluring to browsers fifty years hence? Will the name Martin Amis strike the same note as E. M. Forster?

Camilla's, Eastbourne

Selling second-hand books runs in the Francombe family. Camilla Francombe, together with Stuart Broad, formerly a lecturer at Worthing College, owns the shop in Grove Road, a short walk from Eastbourne station, and her mother, Kim Francombe, has given her own name to a Worthing shop, as already recorded in these pages. Camilla's first opened in Brighton in 1976 and moved to Eastbourne nine years later, to a corner site where there has been a bookshop since the 1940s. And it is chock-a-block; the frontage, with its striped awning and boxes of paperbacks, seems to bulge; and, inside, I can truthfully say I have never seen so many books – half a million of them – in a comparable space.

On the door is displayed a cutting from *The Spectator*, with Christopher Hawtree passing his verdict on Camilla's, as follows: "A chest-high Great Dane greets visitors here, but his jaws are milder than the false-gums pink of the shop's carrier-bags. The stock is spread across three floors, sometimes expensive but generally reasonable; along with lesser shops round the corner in South Street, it is Eastbourne's saving grace."

There used to be two Great Danes until one died, leaving Rock, who mostly stays at home now. With Camilla herself in the background, a Great Dane peers out red-eyed from between stacks of books on the shop's postcard; and on the ground floor, within arm's length of the inquiry desk, there are four shelves of books about dogs, including, besides all the usual ones about individual breeds, Laura Thompson's paean to greyhound racing, *The Dogs*. I asked Camilla

Camilla's, chock-a-block shop in Eastbourne. Spot the Great Dane in the foreground.

whether any well-known people come to the shop and she mentioned Denis Healey and the Reverend Ian Paisley, whose dog exchanges cards with Rock.

I looked for something by A. Alvarez, without success. His best book in a varied output may yet prove to be *The Savage God*, a study of suicide, published in 1971. I have known three people who committed suicide. One was the gossip columnist on the first newspaper I worked for. He jumped from a high window in New Orleans – why was never discovered. Another, a woman in her forties, took an overdose because, it was believed, of her failure, or inability, to have children. The third was a bowler with marital difficulties who went down to Ramsgate one evening, boarded the Ostend ferry, and, a mile or so out, jumped overboard carrying a case containing his four bowls. I learned of, though never met, a fourth, a neighbour, who was diagnosed with terminal illness and left a note on his kitchen table, saying, "You will find me in the garage."

I glanced through *Cliches*, by Betty Kirkpatrick, because the subject is of perennial interest to journalists; almost purchased *The Greenwood Hat*, J. M. Barrie's early autobiography, which has a foreword by Stanley Baldwin; and failed to unearth *Hit Hard and Enjoy It*, by T. C. "Dickie" Dodds, whose obituary appeared in *The Times* and the *Daily Telegraph* the week before I visited Camilla's. Cricketing readers of a certain age will remember Dodds, a vicar's son, as a dashing post-war batsman for Essex who hit sixes in accordance with his religious convictions. He believed the game to be "a reflection of the greatest Creator."

In South Street Alan and Tania Gibbard have an attractive shop, comprising a ground floor and basement, which they took over in 1993. There has been a bookshop there since 1909. The first owner was J. G. Glover and he was followed by his daughter, Joyce, who wrote children's books; she sold the business to Raymond Smith and his wife in 1963; and now the Gibbards are upholding a solid tradition.

There are twelve shelves, floor to ceiling, on the ground floor, with literature and natural history prominent. Seeing a first edition of *London's Natural History*, by R. S. R. Fitter, reminded me that when

I was a boy in Aberdeen an aunt and uncle who lived in London sent me a copy as a Christmas present, although I knew nothing then of either London or natural history, let alone a combination of the two. This did not strike me as curious at the time, but it does now. Downstairs I dipped into Marjorie Bowen's novel *The Viper of Milan*, with its introductory note by Graham Greene beginning, tantalisingly, "Perhaps it is only in childhood that books have any deep influence on our lives," and going on to say that reading it, at the age of fourteen, was what determined him to be a writer.

Brookes, Brighton

Noel Brookes greeted me in courtly fashion when I introduced myself at the entrance to his shop just past the clock tower in Queen's Road; and when I explained my mission he mentioned one or two books about second-hand bookshops which he thought might interest me, beginning with a paperback entitled *Bookworm Droppings*. This is an anthology of absurd remarks made by customers and includes examples from shops I toured while writing this book – Ken Spelman of York, Richard Way of Henley, and of course Mr Brookes himself, one of whose customers put this problem to him: "I want a copy of Plato's *Republic* but I don't know who it's by."

Knock or Ring, a novel with a bookish theme by Michael Nelson, published in the late 1950s, was unknown to me; likewise *The Travelling Bookshop* by an American novelist whose name Mr Brookes could not recall but whose book sounded out of the common run: the story of someone who loaded a horse and cart with books and travelled to parts of America where there were no bookshops. (In the light of later knowledge, it occurred to me that Mr Brookes may have been thinking of Christopher Morley's *Parnassus on Wheels*.)

Mr Brookes comes from the village of Kinver, near Stourbridge, and his shop, untidy yet inviting, has occupied its Brighton home since 1981. It is open all year except Christmas Day and Boxing Day, and unusual among its specialities is Polish literature. Needing to verify a quotation from Graham Greene, I found it on a shelf here – in *Brighton*

Rock, with its opening words: "Hale knew, before he had been in Brighton three hours, that they meant to murder him." Though not visible, another notable Brighton novel, Patrick Hamilton's *The West Pier*, was probably nearby.

Colin Page Antiquarian Books in Duke Street originated in Lewes in 1969 and after the move to Brighton was bought out by John Loska, a Sussex University graduate, Brighton born and bred, who has retained Colin Page's name for business purposes. The older books (and that sometimes means fifteenth century) are at street level, with the general books in the basement, reached by a narrow spiral staircase in ironwork.

Down there I saw Rex Bellamy's *The Peak District Companion*. When I worked with the author he was tennis correspondent of *The Times*, and a brilliant writer, able to turn his hand to any sport that took his fancy. The Peak District book reflects his lifelong passion for hill-walking. I also noted *A Year's Residence in the United States of America*, by William Cobbett, described by J. E. Morpurgo in his introduction as "the preface to *Rural Rides*," and *War Report*, Trevor Royle's account of the work of war correspondents from the Crimea to the Falklands. Despite never having been a soldier – or perhaps because of it – Royle has a fascination with the military, and he wrote an admirable social history of National Service, *The Best Years of Their Lives*.

All Bull, edited by the novelist B. S. Johnson, takes a subjective approach to the same subject, with twenty-four former conscripts such as Michael Holroyd, David Hockney and (memorably) Jeff Nuttall recalling their stint in uniform. Read both books and you get a rounded view. I have never regretted doing National Service. Starting with homesickness and confusion it had its unpleasant moments, but those were to be expected. The effects of the whole experience, whether a waste of time or not, were more beneficial than otherwise.

James Savery and his wife Sarah own a large shop on Ditchling Road, with an estimated stock in its nine rooms of a quarter of a million volumes. Mrs Savery's mother-in-law and sister-in-law run the antiques shop on the opposite side of the road where the whole business began in 1990. There is a healthy exchange with overseas customers.

In Trafalgar Street, adjacent to the railway station, you will find two second-hand bookshops – the Trafalgar and the Rainbow. The former specialises in horse-racing, and in the latter I saw, on a chair, a copy of what is believed to be the first Western novel, Owen Wister's *The Virginian*, anticipating everyone from Zane Grey to Louis L'Amour. *The Virginian* was published by Macmillan in 1902 and filmed in 1929 with Gary Cooper. In the cinema now Westerns are so rarely shown that you might think the *genre* had never existed. They appear regularly on television, but the small screen emasculates them, which rules them out for me. I have written to the National Film Theatre to protest about this neglect of what Dilys Powell called "perhaps the one completely achieved form of the cinema".

Sanctuary, Lyme Regis

If you want something startlingly different, make haste to Lyme Regis and the Sanctuary Bookshop on Broad Street. Jane Austen wrote part of *Persuasion* there, John Fowles lives up the road, and the town was a favourite with people like Tennyson and G. K. Chesterton; but these are predictable facts. The shop's proprietor, Bob Speer, a retired physics lecturer from Imperial College, London, has more curious things to show.

Upstairs, walled in by books, is what he calls a book-lover's b&b, comprising bedroom, living-room, private bathroom, colour television, and a choice of breakfasts. It is a no-smoking area, the tariffs are about £20 a night low season and £24 mid-season, and Mr Speer's Japanese wife, Mariko, is in charge of the flat. Elsewhere in this warren of a building are an internet room, and a basement with a roof so low you cannot stand up straight, two deep armchairs, a log fire, books priced at £1 or less, and copies of the *National Geographic Magazine* dating back to 1918.

The day we were there, on the way to visit relatives at Brampford Speke near Exeter, the ground-floor counter was flanked by a pianola,

Bob Speer performing on the pianola in his Sanctuary Bookshop in Lyme Regis.

which had just been sold for £1,250, and a Paris organ from 1860. Half jokingly, we asked Mr Speer to give us a tune on the pianola, and he obliged, *vivace*, with Lara's theme from the film *Doctor Zhivago*, a Christmas carol or two, and some jazz. Altogether, his shop is more than a shop, it is an experience.

Michael Foot and Jeremy Paxman have been among the customers of the Dartmoor Bookshop, in the market town of Ashburton, which was opened in 1974 by Evelyn Lowell in the back room of her husband Harold's paper shop on North Street. When the bookshop was moved to its present premises in Kingsbridge Lane in 1982, Paul Heatley happened to come along on the opening day with books to sell, and he now runs the shop in partnership with his wife Barbara, one of the Lowells' two daughters, the other daughter, Anne, also helping out behind the reception desk.

The Pendulum Years, Bernard Levin's idiosyncratic survey of the 1960s, was there, and you should relish his account of the national outcry caused by BBC Radio's decision to drop *The Dales*. The deed was done, of course, as all the world knows, and Levin summed it up, thus: "And so they passed over, and all the teacups tinkled for them on the other side."

I saw collected editions of Joseph Conrad's novels and the *Arabian Nights*, and first editions of Helen Thomas's two haunting books about her relationship with the poet Edward Thomas: *As It Was* and *World Without End*. Sir William Haley when he was Editor of *The Times* wrote a weekly column about books, under the pen-name Oliver Edwards, and he had this to say of the closing pages of *World Without End*:

"He (Thomas) joined up in July, 1915, and was killed in April, 1917. Of his final leave at Christmas, his wife has written in a way that warns all others off the ground. There are few passages more moving in English literature. The homely scene, the children being bathed in front of the fire, the reading from Shelley, the last cup of tea in bed the next morning, the leaving of the poems, there is everything here for tears. And I am not ashamed to say that as I read the pages for possibly the twentieth time they still come."

John Bartlett, a classically trained actor, works three days a week in

Joel Segal's shop in Fore Street, Topsham, and spends most of his remaining time writing one-man shows that he performs himself, often in stately homes. He did one called *That Tiger Life* for the centenary of Oscar Wilde's death. A Hampshire man, he has lived in Devon for over thirty years, and says there is a long tradition of actors working in bookshops. Mr Segal lives opposite the shop but rarely appears in it as he concentrates on buying stock.

Natural history always makes an interesting shelf and Segal's had *My Birds*, by W. H. Davies, the Supertramp autobiographer. It is more anecdotal than ornithological. And I saw *Suffolk Scene*, by Julian Tennyson, a great-grandson of the poet, who was killed in Burma, in the last year of the war, by a Japanese mortar bomb.

Broadhurst, Southport

Charles Kenyon Broadhurst was working for W. H. Smith when he borrowed £3,000 from his mother-in-law and opened the Market Street shop that bears his name in 1926. Later there was a second shop in the Liverpool suburb of Waterloo, but it was bombed in the 1939-45 war and never reopened. A photographic memory is an asset in any line of work and Charles Broadhurst had one, so that he had only to touch a book to remember it. He rose to be president of the Antiquarian Booksellers' Association and died in 1986 at the age of ninety, having continued to come in to the shop every day almost to the end.

The present proprietor, and he is only the second in nearly eighty years, is Laurens Hardman, a Liverpudlian and lifelong bibliophile. Getting started had not been easy for him because his father did not consider bookselling to be a proper job, and so they agreed to compromise. The son would try banking for a year and if he did not like it he could leave and do as he wanted. So it came about that he joined Broadhurst's in 1968 as the equivalent of an office boy, sweeping the floors and making the tea.

In a shop with a warm and friendly atmosphere, new books are on the ground floor; with the second-hand stock filling the other rooms upstairs. There is a staff of six full-time and four part-time, and the specialities include modern first editions, children's books and private press books. The ubiquitous Drif approved of Broadhurst's, calling it "the Jack Buchanan of booksellers." "I still haven't worked out exactly what he meant," Mr Hardman says.

I asked about top prices and Mr Hardman recalled the fraction over £20,000 paid by an English buyer for a fourth-folio Shakespeare. I was interested in a first edition of *Oriental Assembly*, the miscellaneous writings of T. E. Lawrence, published in 1939; and in Rider Haggard, who had two shelves to himself. Among personal favourites of mine was James Agate's *Shorter Ego*, one of the better examples of that over-worked *genre*, the diary.

The handsome boulevard of Lord Street is a short distance from Broadhurst's and that is where, opposite the town hall, you will find the Kernaghans' bookshop, on the balcony of Wayfarers' Arcade; this is the only privately owned arcade in Southport and as such it has no high-street department stores, all the shops being independent.

Bryan Kernaghan comes from Belfast and his wife, Alwyn, from Blackburn, and before going into the book trade in the 1980s they spent six years in a residential school in the Himalayas, Alwyn teaching children with special needs and Bryan working on the extra-curricular and pastoral side. You pass bargain boxes on your approach to their shop, which is open-plan, with bays and nooks as subject areas; and at one end is a room with an armchair and a fire, and shelves replete with first editions of militaria and signed copies of theatre books.

I noted a United Kingdom first edition of *Lolita* and, in the main part of the shop, a copy of *Only a Game?*, Eamon Dunphy's diary of a professional footballer, published in 1976. Dunphy played for Millwall and the Republic of Ireland and his book when it came out was immediately welcomed as far superior to the usual "ghost"-written pap about the game. I went to a rugby-playing school, and soccer, with its grotesquely overpaid "superstars" flickering to and fro, to and fro, and ninety-nine times out of a hundred failing to put the ball in the net, bores me. But I have read and enjoyed John Moynihan's *The Soccer Syndrome* and Nick Hornby's *Fever Pitch*, and J. P. W. Mallalieu's re-creation of the 1953 F. A. Cup final – Stanley

Matthews's final – in *Very Ordinary Sportsman* is the most moving description of a football occasion I have read.

". . . For the last three minutes of the match, while the sun was beginning to draw deep shadows across the turf, nobody at Wembley who had a seat used it, and no one who had a voice failed to use it. The roar was unbroken and of a pitch so high and almost hysterical that it was unlike any football noise I had ever heard before. It was more like a wail of exaltation that one can sometimes hear at meetings of the more emotional religious sects in the United States, and as it continued, I felt an inevitableness about the coming climax . . ."

Castle, Colchester

Robert Green owns three second-hand bookshops in East Anglia, namely the Castle, the Treasure Chest in Felixstowe, and Blake's Books in Woodbridge. He is the Castle's second proprietor, the first having been Tony Doncaster, a Sheffield man and former printer, who founded it in George Street in 1948. He had worked as a dogsbody at the Hogarth Press before the war and in Foyle's after demobilisation from the Royal Navy. The shop moved more than once until settling in its present home in Osborne Street, a short walk from Colchester Town railway station.

It occupies two floors and upstairs I found what amounted to the collected works of Daisy Ashford, whose famous book is *The Young Visiters*. She wrote it in a twopenny notebook when she was nine and it turned up years afterwards among her mother's papers. A friend showed it to Frank Swinnerton, he in turn showed it to J. M. Barrie, and it was published in 1919 with a preface by Barrie, who called it "her sublime work."

The Castle also stocked *A Short Story of Love and Marriage*, *The True History of Leslie Woodcock*, *Where Love Lies Deepest*, and *The Hangman's Daughter*, all written by Daisy Ashford by the time she was thirteen; and on the same shelf was her sister Angela's *The Jealous Governes*, with the spelling error in her title matching the one in *The Young Visiters*. There are numerous such errors, all left intact, in the text of *The Young*

Visiters and they add to rather than subtract from the vivid style of the tale, in a way bearing out George Orwell's perhaps tongue-in-cheek dictum that grammar and syntax do not really matter provided the meaning is clear.

I came away from the Castle with a purchase, *The Unquiet Grave*, Cyril Connolly's "word cycle" under the pen-name Palinurus. There are French and Latin bits in it, but they are easily skipped. As Connolly does not bother to translate them for me, I shall not bother to learn a foreign vocabulary for him, or his ghost. The book is a hedonistic mixture of diary and meditation and quotation, the subject-matter marriage, writing, travel, and much else. "What is the *point* of Cyril Connolly?" Anthony Powell once inquired. A possible answer is that Connolly considered himself to be pointless, unable, partly through indolence, to fulfil what he saw as the writer's true function by producing a masterpiece. "All excursions into journalism, broad-casting, propaganda and writing for the films, however grandiose, are doomed to disappointment," he declared. "To put of our best into these forms is another folly, since thereby we condemn good ideas as well as bad to oblivion."

After leaving the Castle bookshop, I walked through Priory Street to East Hill, where the premises of Greyfriars Books are to be found in a surprisingly large basement of three rooms, with Barry Ellam an obliging assistant. He made tea for me while outlining the history of the shop, which was established in 1983 by Roy Taylor, a retired industrial chemist and, like Mr Ellam, a Yorkshireman. When Mr Taylor died, his wife Pauline and their son Simon retained the shop, and if you want a good broad stock tidily displayed you should drop into Greyfriars.

"We deal in most subjects," Mr Ellam said, "but one thing we don't touch is real-life crime, about people like the Kray brothers. It could attract the wrong sort of customer."

I have read only two Booker Prize-winning novels, Anita Brookner's *Hotel du Lac* and *The Remains of the Day*, by Kazuo Ishiguro, and Greyfriars stocked the Ishiguro, as well as another of his, *The Unconsoled*. One of the fascinations of Ishiguro, as it is of Joseph Conrad, is his way with a language not his own. With Ishiguro the result of this music-making on an unfamiliar instrument is a sort of cool, hypnotic formality (reflecting Japanese politeness?) that draws you on and on to the end, even when, as in the case of *The Unconsoled*, you are sometimes baffled as to what it all means.

Thornton's, Oxford

Blackwell's is to Oxford what Foyle's is to the Charing Cross Road, but with only one floor of second-hand stock it is not the equal of Thornton's, Oxford's oldest independent bookshop, at the other end of Broad Street. Thornton's has three floors, and has been there longer, too – since 1863, in fact, twenty-eight years after being started in Magdalen Street, with capital of £260, by Joseph Thornton, the son of a nonconformist Essex clergyman.

Members of the Thornton family carried on the business well into the twentieth century, drawing their customers mainly from the University, and in 1983 they amalgamated with another Oxford shop, Holdan Books, specialists in European languages, which doubled their stock to a hundred thousand volumes. Two years later the rare books department was opened on the top floor, next to a Russian room.

There was a cloud on the horizon when I visited Thornton's for the first time, shortly before Christmas. After such a long period of stability, Willem Meeuws, the proprietor, and his staff were facing up to the likelihood of having to move to a smaller site in a part of the city where there the rent would be less prohibitive and the parking easier. Some of the charming intimacy of the late nineteenth-century shop would certainly be lost in the upheaval, not to mention one of Oxford's cultural landmarks. It was good, therefore, to see the shop still in its traditional incarnation, and to pass on one's heartfelt best wishes.

I read that a literary journal called *The Spirit Lamp* was published by James Thornton towards the end of the nineteenth century, edited by Lord Alfred Douglas and with contributors such as Oscar Wilde and Max Beerbohm, and that it was revived in 1986 to mark the shop's one hundred and fiftieth anniversary. I also learned that scenes in the

TV adaptation of Evelyn Waugh's *Brideshead Revisited* had been filmed in Thornton's in 1981.

I came across a surprise on the ground floor – *Mightier than the Sword*, Alphonse Courlander's Fleet Street novel, published in 1912 and praised by Sir William Haley in one of his *Times* columns referred to earlier. He wrote that Courlander saw a journalist's life in terms not of romance but of tragedy, and quoted a passage from Courlander saying that Fleet Street "lures you like a siren, coaxing with soft promises of prizes to be wrested from it: you shall be the favoured of the gods, and you become Sisyphus, rolling his stone eternally, day after day. Here are the things of life that you covet, they shall be yours, says the Street; and you are Tantalus, reaching out everlastingly, and grasping nothing, until your heart is parched within you. You shall be strong and mighty, it says, sapping your strength like Delilah, until you pull down the pillars of hope, and fall buried beneath the reckless ruins of your career."

My next stop was Unsworth's shop in Turl Street, not far from Thornton's, and they had a fat book entitled *Exploring Harry Potter*, nearly five hundred pages of analysis and so forth by Elizabeth D. Schafer, with this caution on the front cover: "NOT approved by J. K. Rowling." It is in a series of "Beacham's Sourcebooks For Teaching Young Adult Fiction," and when I told my wife, who is a teacher, about it, she remarked with feeling: "Why don't they let children just read and enjoy without analysing everything?" Unsworth's advertised itself with a quotation from *Time Out* magazine pasted on the wall: "The great thing about this shop is that it reeks of academia."

After lunch at the Mitre, I discovered that Sanders in the High Street (founded 1840), despite still having an entry in Sheppard's directory, had ceased book-dealing in the 1990s and now concentrated on maps and prints. Roy Harley Lewis tells us in his book browsers' guide that Sanders used to have its resident ghost, with cleaning ladies claiming to have been tapped on the shoulder by "someone" who was "not seen" and sales assistants seeing a blurred monkish apparition.

I finished at Waterfield's, also in the High. Robin Waterfield was a missionary in Iran before opening his shop in 1973. He retired some years ago and the business passed into the hands of John Stephens, a Cambridge graduate, who had worked for the Inland Revenue. My wife being a dog-lover, I bought *"The Dear Dogs"*, by John Galsworthy's wife Ada, for her Christmas.

The Bookshop, Cambridge

Second-hand booksellers are a dying breed in Cambridge, one of them said to me, and I saw some of the evidence of this for myself. Galloway & Porter in Sidney Street, a century-old firm where Charles Traylen, of Guildford, served his apprenticeship some eighty years ago, now deals to a large extent in publishers' remainders. The second-hand stock at David's in St Edward's Passage (founded by a Parisian, Gustave David, in 1896) is negligible, although it does have a good antiquarian room. Heffer's, Cambridge's best-known bookstore, which originated in a stationery shop in Fitzroy Street in 1876, closed its second-hand department in 1973, but at least this has been started up again in a small way in Trinity Street.

Hugh Hardinge, who also has a stall in the market, and Peter Bright share the running of The Bookshop in Magdalene Street, and it is the real thing, not an uneasy compromise between new and old books, with its medium stock covering a wide subject range. There were bound issues of *Punch*, from 1888 to 1971, in the window, a long row of King Penguins, and, at the rear of the shop, the three *Music in London* volumes of Bernard Shaw, a reminder that his collected musical and theatrical journalism – eight volumes of it, I think – never fails to entertain and educate. I would not mind very much if I never saw another Shaw play, but I would mind if his writings on Beethoven and Shakespeare were somehow to be lost to the world.

In his engrossing biography of Shaw, which one critic believed would find as secure a place among the classics as Eckermann's *Goethe* and Boswell's *Johnson*, Hesketh Pearson wrote.

"Shaw discoursed on many matters, including music, under the pseudonym of Corno di Bassetto, the name of an instrument that gave forth melancholy sounds suitable for a funeral; and as Shaw was out to kill the technical jargon which passed for musical criticism, he could not have hit upon a more appropriate title. 'Seriousness,' he wrote, 'is the small man's affectation of bigness'; and the crushing boredom with which the average person reads programme-notes, books and newspaper columns on music was completely absent while Shaw was diverting himself on the subject. He wrote in order to be read by people who did not know the difference between a crotchet and a quaver; . . . . and it is pleasant to record that while the Parrys, Stanfords, Mackenzies and other musical bigwigs of that time were holding up their hands in shocked amazement, the greatest of English composers, Edward Elgar, then a young and struggling teacher of music, was enjoying Shaw's quips so heartily that when they met one another in late life the composer was able to quote many passages which the critic had long forgotten."

A bookshop may be the ideal home for a ghost, with the massed works of imagination on the shelves preying on the imaginations of owners and customers. Oxford had Sanders, while Cambridge has The Haunted Bookshop, in St Edward's Passage, across the road from King's College. Asked about her experience of the local ghost, Sarah Key, joint owner of the shop with Phil Salin, said she was convinced she had seen someone going upstairs but when she went to look the room was empty.

There is ample food for children's imaginations in the shop, which opened in 1960 and specialises in juvenilia. Dorita Fairlie-Bruce's Dimsie books filled two shelves, and Enid Blyton, Beatrix Potter and company were there, too. The whole of the upper floor is given over to the sort of books that children made a beeline for in the distant days before the sad appropriation of their lives by television.

I left The Haunted Bookshop having discovered and bought, at the last moment, *The Haunted Bookshop*, by an American novelist Christopher Morley, which is about a second-hand bookshop in Brooklyn. The coincidence prompted me to buy, though not before opening the book at random to see if I liked the author's style and general drift. If there were any doubts, they vanished when I read this: "If your mind needs phosphorus, try *Trivia*, by Logan Pearsall Smith.

If your mind needs a whiff of strong air, blue and cleansing, from hill-tops and primrose valleys, try *The Story of My Heart*, by Richard Jefferies."

Pearsall Smith was an American man of letters who became a British subject: a miniaturist at heart, eternally polishing aphorisms and short essays. A few years ago I stumbled in a Lancashire shop on his *All Trivia*, the complete edition, with a foreword by Gore Vidal, who wrote that "(Logan) retells legends and composes entire novels and biographies in a page, while producing eternal wisdom as well as life-enhancing malice in a series of phrases."

Here is Pearsall Smith on the subject of joy:

"Sometimes at breakfast, sometimes in a train or empty bus, or on the moving stairs at Charing Cross, I am happy; the earth turns to gold, and life becomes a magical adventure. Only yesterday, travelling alone to Sussex, I became light-headed with this sudden joy. The train seemed to rush to its adorable destination through a world newborn in brightness, bathed in a beautiful element, fresh and clear as on the morning of Creation. Even the coloured photographs of the South Coast watering-places in the railway carriage shone with the light of Paradise upon them. Brighton faced me; next to it divine Southsea beckoned; and oh, the esplanade at Ryde! Then I saw the beach at Sidmouth, the Tilly Whim caves near Swanage; – was it in those unhaunted caves, or amid the tumult of life which hums about the Worthing bandstand, that I should find Bliss in its quintessence?

"Or on the pier at St Peter Port perhaps, in the Channel Islands, amid that crowd who watch in eternal ecstasy the ever-arriving, never-disembarking Weymouth steamer?"

Barely Read Books, Westerham

Ross Williams was eight years old when reading the Biggles stories gave him his love of books, and he has now opened a shop facing the Churchill statue on Westerham Green and dealing in second-hand and nearly new stock. This is the fulfilment of an ambition and he came to it after working as a publisher's rep., travelling around Kent, Surrey and Sussex for Hodder & Stoughton, Macdonalds and Little, Brown, and for Eunice Watkins in her Maidstone bookshop. "I'm as much a Biggles fan as ever," he says, "I think there are over a hundred Biggles books and I'm still collecting and selling them."

He made a flattering observation about book-buyers. In his experience of postal dealing they always pay on time, or at any rate within a month or two of purchase, and he never worries if a cheque is slow to arrive: he has complete faith that sooner or later it will.

He said that the books on display in the shop form only a small percentage of his total stock. *Kilvert's Diary*, in William Plomer's abridged edition, was a familiar sight on the crowded shelves, although I have glimpsed the rarer three-volume sets several times on my travels. *In Your Garden With Percy Thrower* reminded me of a visit my wife and I made to the Shrewsbury show over twenty years ago, when Thrower, with his champion fuchsias, was in his prime. It was a Saturday and very hot, and as we sat in the bus in the evening waiting to return to our guest-house in Church Stretton, we watched dozens of exhibitors going home hidden beneath their plants and ferns, like a moving forest.

Alan Taylor-Smith used to have a bookshop in Westerham High Street, but he now does business from a storeroom, mainly in Churchilliana, Chartwell being a mile or so from Westerham. Both my parents admired Churchill, my mother to the point of hero-worship, and they possessed numerous books by or about him; but the only books of his that I have read are *Great Contemporaries*, *My Early Life* and *Painting as a Pastime*.

Next door to Barely Read is a coffee shop called Tiffins, which, along with Browsers at Lingfield in Surrey, is used by David Neal as an extra outlet for books. Browsers has much the larger and more varied selection of the two, and its food is good. Mr Neal has two shops in Oxted, just over the border in Surrey – namely Second-hand Bookshop and Books in the Basement, both founded in the 1990s and both in Station Road, with access by a subway.

Second-hand Bookshop is a true shop of its kind, with a bias towards non-fiction, but Books in the Basement, situated beneath a furnishing store, has the bigger stock, some nine thousand volumes. I saw novels by C. S. Forester and Hammond Innes, both of whom, with their storytelling gift, helped me make the transition from youthful to adult reading, although for some reason I never tried the Hornblower stories.

H. M. Gilbert & Son, Southampton

The Gilbert family have been booksellers since 1859 and the present proprietor, Richard Gilbert, is the fifth generation. The founder was Henry March Gilbert, a writer, printer and bookseller, who moved to Southampton from Halstead in Essex to escape religious harassment; he claimed that sectarian rivalry in Halstead was so bitter that, because of his nonconformist opinions, the local Anglicans set up one of their own men in business as a bookseller.

The firm had several homes in Southampton, latterly in Above Bar, before settling in Portland Street in 1939, at number 2½ – a Victorian postal curiosity that amuses visitors and prompts some sceptical correspondents to "correct" the address to 2a or 21. Like Above Bar, Portland Street was bombed during the second world war, but the Gilbert building was unscathed. A branch in Winchester, which was opened in The Square in 1904 by Henry Gilbert's younger son, Owen, closed down in 1999.

When the shop was in Above Bar, T. E. Lawrence, who lodged nearby, used to drop in incognito, creating a potentially embarrassing situation, for Owen Gilbert knew who Lawrence was and Lawrence knew that he knew. The Portland Street premises have six rooms upstairs where I spent some time looking into a reissue of *The Irish Guards in the Great War*, which Rudyard Kipling undertook to write after his eighteen-year-old son, John, had been killed while serving with the regiment at Loos. It was first published in 1923 and is now seen as a rediscovered masterpiece. Kipling himself said: "This will be my great work. It is done with agony and bloody sweat."

From Gilbert's I made my way to a comparatively new shop, Peter Rhodes, formerly known as Open Hand Books, in Portswood Road. Mr Rhodes has a degree from King Alfred's College, Winchester, where his subjects were geography and American studies, and he worked in the Oxfam bookshop in Winchester before taking up bookselling seriously in Southampton with an initial stock of four hundred volumes. That figure now runs into thousands, with most categories on the ground floor and music and theatre in a basement at the rear.

We discussed Drif ("He's something of a legend, isn't he?") and American bookshops, which Mr Rhodes admires, having toured those of New England, and I then explored his stock, noting *The Oregon Trail*, Francis Parkman's account of prairie and mountain life, which I remember from my youth, and Norman Collins's novel *London Belongs to Me*. I must have seen the film of this when it came out in 1948, with Richard Attenborough and Alastair Sim, but although I never read the entire book I have often returned to the preface; with its artfully conversational tone, it is, I think, worth a place in any London anthology.

"Every city has its something" (Collins wrote). "Rome has St Peter's. Peking has its Summer Palace. Moscow has the Kremlin. In Madrid there's the Prado. In New York there's the Empire State. Constantinople has St Sophia. Cairo has Shepheard's. Paris has got the Eiffel Tower. Sydney has a bridge. Naples is content with its bay. Cape Town has Table Mountain. Benares is famous for its burning ghats. Pisa has a Leaning Tower. Toledo has a bull-ring. Stockholm has a Town Hall. Vancouver has a view. But London . . . London . . . What *is* it that London's got?

"Well, there's St Paul's Cathedral. But St Peter's could put it into its pocket. There's Westminster Abbey. But there are Abbeys everywhere; they're dotted all over Europe. There's the Tower. Admittedly the dungeons are convincing, but as a castle it's nothing. Not beside Edinburgh or Caernarvon. Even Tower Hill isn't really a hill; it's only an incline. Then there are the Houses of Parliament and the Law Courts. But they're merely so much Victorian Gothic – all turrets and arches and railings and things. . . ."

Get a copy of the book and find out what it is that London's got.

Academy, Southsea

Southsea has a number of footnotes in literary annals. Conan Doyle wrote his first Sherlock Holmes story, *A Study in Scarlet*, while in medical practice there; H. G. Wells worked as a draper's assistant in the town; and the boy Kipling spent six unhappy years lodging in what he called "the house of desolation" while his parents were in India. Most notable of all, Charles Dickens was born in the neighbourhood.

The Academy bookshop in Marmion Road has a large collection of books by or about Dickens and the owner, Bill Robinson, pulled out some of the more unusual of them to show me. There was a two-volume *Pickwick* printed entirely in shorthand, something called *The Pic Nic Papers*, composed by various hands and edited by Dickens himself, and *With Dickens in Yorkshire*, by T. P. Cooper, amending the common view of Dickens as a man and writer circumscribed by London and Kent. There was also a two-volume first edition of *Little Dorrit* priced at £185.

The shorthand *Pickwick* led on to a corner shelf of books on shorthand itself, including *Transactions of the First International Shorthand Congress*, which was held in London in 1887, and a copy of the primer with which I tried to learn Pitman long ago; I never exceeded sixty words a minute. Another of Mr Robinson's specialities is theology and he told me that he sells a Bible a day.

Mr Robinson, a Mancunian, spent twenty-three years serving in Royal Navy battleships all over the world before entering the book trade in 1976, initially at Lee-on-Solent. He estimated his stock at 150,000, admitting that he had a problem knowing where to put it all. It is a problem solved at least partly by a Salisbury firm called In Gear who over the years have relieved him of 100,000 unwanted books, some of which have reappeared, more as decoration than as reading matter, on public-house and restaurant shelves.

The Abbey in Fawcett Road was opened by Nick Purkis, formerly a north London schoolteacher, in 1986, when there was no staircase and almost no shelving. By dint of a lot of hard work, and a starting stock of eight hundred, which is now more like twenty-five thousand, he has transformed it into a spick and span shop on two floors with a broad range of subjects, three of the most popular, fiction, biography and sport, being upstairs.

Mr Purkis made tea and let me have a copy of the 1992-93 edition of *Drif's guide*, describing Drif as "the Egon Ronay of the book business." I was about to leave when he mentioned the chess club that he runs in his shop: it is, however, not a club as such, simply a meeting-place for enthusiasts of the game, some of county standard, who drop in when they feel like it to pass an hour or complete a move. An art historian from the local university came in to do this while I was there, and Mr Purkis brought out the board with the pieces exactly where they had left them at the end of their previous session.

The Jade Mountain in Highland Road was closed, but Mr Purkis directed me to the Adelphi, a small shop in Albert Road, where I saw a copy of *The Kingdom by the Sea*, Paul Theroux's account of his odyssey round the coast of Britain in the summer of 1982. Theroux is a much sharper writer than Bill Bryson, another American who has lived in and written about this country, and I admire the concentrated energy required to do what Theroux presumably did – travel on foot and by rail day after day for weeks and write it all up every night (or early morning).

Incidentally, his notorious chapter on Aberdeen, my home city, incensed many Aberdonians but not me; but then I am not a typical Aberdonian, having had an English mother and having lived in England since 1962. Theroux loathed many things about Aberdeen in its oil-capital aspect, and had some unfortunate experiences there, but his criticisms are laced with black humour and he ends by enumerating the many things, the "ordinary" things, that he liked, from the bread and the fish and the flower gardens to the way the streets were frequently full of seagulls.

Arriving home, I picked up *The Times* and read a letter from Phil James, a second-hand book dealer in Horsham, saying that Dickens, Shakespeare and Jane Austen led his classics league table of sales by an overwhelming margin, with Kipling, Hardy and Tennyson next. Bunyan and Keats came last. He cannot sell Walter Scott for love or money, and Shaw was another "sticker", which surprised him.

Readers Rest, Lincoln

I found five second-hand bookshops in Lincoln: Harlequin Gallery, Golden Goose Books, Smallwood Books (alternatively known as the Bookshop in the Prison), Bookshop at the Plain, and Readers Rest. Readers Rest is on Steep Hill (steep is an understatement, so be warned) and it has, in addition to the main shop, a book hall on the opposite side of the road that is open for business on Saturdays.

Nick Warwick was in his twentieth year as the proprietor of Readers Rest when I met him, and his stock is a mixture of second-hand, nearly new and new. "I don't have very old or antiquarian books," he said. I did not buy anything, though I was tempted by Siegfried Sassoon's war poems, but in passing I enjoyed the odds and ends of anecdote and information that Mr Warwick over a longish period had copied out and pinned up on the walls. George Orwell worked in a Hampstead bookshop between the wars and at the far end of the Lincoln shop I found on display an extract from his essay "Bookshop Memories" in which he mentions "the dear old lady who read such a nice book in 1897 and wonders if you can find her a copy. Unfortunately she doesn't remember the title or the author's name or what the book is about, but she does remember it had a red cover."

Orwell also wrote: "One thing that strikes you is how completely the 'classical' English novelists have dropped out of favour . . . At the mere sight of a nineteenth-century novel people say 'Oh but that's *old*!' Yet it is fairly easy to *sell* Dickens, just as it is always easy to sell Shakespeare. Dickens is one of those authors whom people are 'always meaning to' read and, like the Bible, he is widely known at second hand."

On the factual side you can learn from another of Mr Warwick's cuttings that "John Creasey, after receiving a probable record 743 rejection slips, had 564 books totalling forty million words published from 1932 to his death in 1973." Further decoration in the shop is provided in the form of animal posters with, for example, a cat endorsing the statement: "I never buy second-hand books – one never knows where they've been."

Thomas Smallwood and his father Steven run the Bookshop in the

Prison, which is housed in the old prison building in the grounds of Lincoln Castle. They started in the late 1990s, Mr Smallwood, sen., having already had experience of the book trade in Cirencester. There are two rooms, with a good selection of books in the available space; but the Smallwoods, despite affection for the traditional second-hand bookshop, admit that they see the future more and more in terms of internet-dealing with an entirely different stock.

Seeing Conrad's *Heart of Darkness* was a reminder of the way that that story's title has been taken over by journalists to describe any grim subject, whether appropriate or not. And *Long Day's Journey Into Night*, Eugene O'Neill's play about an authentic heart of darkness in his own family, recalled for me a memorable evening in, I think, the National Theatre when fog rolled and curled across the stage and out into the auditorium, emphasising (in O'Neill's words) the isolation of "the four haunted Tyrones."

Harlequin Gallery and Golden Goose, both owned by Richard West-Skinn on Steep Hill, were originally separate shops but are now one. The Bookshop at the Plain, on West Parade, used to be in Cowley Road, Oxford, but Michael Watts brought it to Lincoln a couple of years ago. He, too, was feeling the pinch of the internet and having to think about a possible move to private premises.

E. M. Forster's description in *Howards End* of Beethoven's fifth symphony is famous; and equally fine and true in its own way, though less familiar, is the essay "The C Minor of That Life" in Forster's *Two Cheers for Democracy*, of which I saw a first edition on Mr Watts's shelves. The music here includes Beethoven's last piano sonata, "with its opening dive into the abyss," an other-worldly piece I would unhesitatingly take to the desert island. Cardus wrote that hearing it for the first time "was my baptism into music as a spiritual fact. I did not understand the language, but I heard the voice."

Portland, Leamington Spa

Smith Street in Warwick is a narrow, gently sloping, rather homely thoroughfare, despite the traffic, and that is where you will find

Duncan Allsop's antiquarian and modern bookshop, established in 1966 and now occupying a seventeenth-century building. Mr Allsop was born in Chesterfield and has spent nearly half a century in bookselling, having trained with an American firm in London before branching out on his own in this conveniently central location. Originally he called his shop the Warwick Castle Bookshop but dropped the title when he kept getting calls from visitors requesting information about things like tours of the castle. His son, Robert, has the Eastgate bookshop farther up Smith Street.

Mr Allsop's stock is varied and he specialises in Warwickshire matters and in sport, particularly real tennis and cricket. I always look closely at cricket books. When I worked for the Aberdeen morning paper in the 1950s, one of the sub-editors, R. T. (Bob) Johnston, published a book of short stories about cricket called *Century of a Lifetime*, for which he also drew the illustrations; he gave me a signed copy. He was crazy about the game and remembered getting autographs when Bradman's Australians played in the north of Scotland in 1938. Before the war he had freelanced in Fleet Street. At the end of the war, while waiting in return home from Burma, he wrote a novel, *Squadron Will Move*, under the pen-name R. A. Forsyth, and that too was published. He was the first novelist I ever met, but since then I have not seen either of his books in the shops, although both, I think, were published by Macmillan.

From Warwick I travelled one stop down the line to Leamington Spa where, against the modern trend, Portland Books is expanding, with a new shop in Warwick Street in the town centre, opening six days a week, in addition to the one in Campion Terrace, which opens on Thursday, Friday and Saturday. The original shop was opened in 1974; Martyn Davies bought the business from Jan Weddup in 1989, having previously worked from home; and the move to Campion Terrace was made in 2000.

The shop stretches a long way back, with an estimated thirty thousand volumes, and a roofed-over yard offering bargains at twenty pence softback and fifty pence hardback. There is a booksearch service; valuations are undertaken and libraries purchased (Mr Davies told me of one such transaction involving eight thousand books); and local authors are sure of a welcome if they want their works advertised in the shop. I saw one of these advertisements for Jean Field's biography of the Victorian poet and man of letters, Walter Savage Landor, who was born in Warwick.

The Sally Bowles/Berlin novels of Christopher Isherwood, and *The American Scene*, by Henry James, were there, the latter a sort of complement to James's *English Hours*, which has a chapter on Warwickshire, with references to Warwick but none to Leamington. Mr Davies has travelled extensively on business in the United States, which prompted me to mention the Strand bookstore in New York. "Powell's in Chicago is even bigger," he said. "It has supermarket-style checkouts, and it makes Hay-on-Wye look like a toyshop." Neither of us said as much, but I fancy that, as far as second-hand bookshops are concerned, at least on this side of the Atlantic, we believe that small is beautiful. I once spent two days in Hay, and bought one book, but I found the whole place too much. Just as you can overeat, so you can overbrowse, inducing exhaustion and even irritation. Some of the Hay shops are more like aircraft hangars, and you can waste valuable time merely walking from one subject to another.

With a possible eye to the future, I bought from Portland *Tales From a Peak District Bookshop*, by a retired Sheffield headteacher, Mike Smith, who ran the High Street Bookshop in Buxton, describing it as "a small piece of paradise." He says: "Bookselling is pleasurable because it is satisfying to see good books going to good homes, but also wrenching because each sale is a book lost from the shelves."

Sterling, Weston-super-Mare

"Under a dark collapsing sky, Weston-super-Mare looked bleak and residential and rather funless," Paul Theroux wrote. "Like Bexhill and Worthing and other places on the south coast it was a large town with the soul of a suburb. And it was in such places that I regretted the endless rows of housefronts and pined for a little vulgarity or something vicious. In Weston-super-Mare I was directed to the 'Waxworks'."

David Nisbet does not pine for a little vulgarity or something vicious. He thinks the town has a lot going for it, which is an oblique way of saying that the civic authorities could do more to promote it. His opinion is worth having because, although he was not born in Weston-super-Mare, he counts himself a Westonian, having lived there a long time.

A Gloucestershire man, he has been in the bookselling business all his life, that is to say for the better part of sixty years, and he now owns Sterling Books in Locking Road, which, if you come by train, can be reached by a short cut through Tesco's car park immediately in front of the station. He started in 1966, working from home, and set up in the present shop in 1984. It is jam-packed with books, concealing heaven knows what treasures, and the only room in the building without them is the toilet, and then only just. "We specialise in everything," Mr Nisbet says. "The stock grows and grows while the space stays the same." When, thinking to make his eyes pop at something outlandish, I told him about the shorthand edition of *Pickwick Papers* that I saw in Southsea, he showed no surprise, saying that he himself had sold shorthand Bibles.

He does bookbinding and picture-framing, there is the customary booksearch service, and the shop is on the internet, with business conducted everywhere from Yatton and Axbridge to Hungary and Australia. Somebody came in and asked for a history of the Somerset Light Infantry. Mr Nisbet could not produce exactly what the man wanted there and then, but he assured him that it should not take too long to track down a book containing the regiment's exploits in the second world war. Having a taste for military history, inherited from my father, who sometimes said he would have liked to have made the army his career, I inquired about Field Marshal Slim's account of the Burma campaign, *Defeat Into Victory*; and in a corner I noticed Noel Barber's *Sinister Twilight* about the fall of Singapore. I used to have a paperback copy of this, but mislaid it, or perhaps lent it to a forgetful friend. It has been my experience over a long period that the people who return books promptly (if at all) to the lender are in a small minority.

There is another bookshop in Weston, not far from the Sterling.

This is the Manna, in Orchard Street, owned by Peter Fairnington. He was listening to Classic FM when I called, which is a good sign up to a point. His stock is smaller than Mr Nisbet's and therefore easier to find your way around, but it looks mostly new or newish, with the second-hand heavily outnumbered.

Afterwards I wandered down to the seafront, bought a cup of tea, and sat on the wall looking across the wide bay, while the donkeys huddled on the sands, families sauntered past, and the sun shone with unexpected warmth for early April.

Two islands

I had no idea of the diversity of the Isle of Wight's literary traditions until I went there for the first time, explored some of its second-hand bookshops, and read Brian Hinton's *Discovering Island Writers* – an indispensable book, in Seamus Heaney's opinion. From Tennyson to J. B. Priestley, from Swinburne to D. H. Lawrence, from Auden to Robert Graves, poets and novelists have lived on or at least visited the island, loved it or otherwise, and left something permanent of themselves there, in word or spirit.

I stayed in Ventnor and found Mr Hinton's book, which was published in 2001, at Ventnor Rare Books in Pier Street. The proprietors here are Nigel Traylen and his wife Teresa, Mr Traylen being the son of Charles Traylen, the Guildford dealer, whose shop was the first stopping-place on my tour over a year ago. Fowler's *The King's English*, dated 1930, caught my eye on the Ventnor shelves, but no more than that; I did not open it. For me, learning to write, and to avoid the commoner mistakes, has been mostly a matter of picking up useful tips from odd informal sources, as a bird picks up crumbs, and consulting books of pedantic advice only in the last resort.

I had intended going on to Freshwater, where there is a shop, Cameron House Books, in Dimbola Lodge, once the home of the Victorian photographer and writer, Julia Margaret Cameron. But I changed my mind at the last moment and went instead to Ryde, which has three shops, including the Ryde Bookshop with overflowing premises in High Street, and Heritage Books in Cross Street. The Heritage is owned by the Reverend Derrick Nearn, who was a missionary in Africa before starting the shop in 1978, and it has an excellent stock fastidiously chosen and displayed around ground floor and basement.

You can get Shakespeare and Dickens anywhere but you have to look much harder for the works of people like George Moore and George Meredith and Walter de la Mare. Mr Nearn had good selections of the latter three, and I bought de la Mare's *Memoirs of a Midget*, which is said to be his masterpiece. I also saw a history of *The New York Times* and a 1941 copy of Jerome K. Jerome's *Three Men in a Boat* containing a note recording the fact that it was the book's one hundred and fifth impression. To sum up: I could have made a dozen or more purchases at the Heritage, but being a believer in the salutary discipline of resisting temptation, made only one.

The southernmost second-hand bookshop in the United Kingdom may be in the Isles of Scilly. It is Waterloo Books, on Harold Wilson's favourite island of St Mary's (we saw his grave by the old parish church), and you will find it in Well Lane, an alleyway near the Hugh Town post office. It is open only on Saturdays in winter (although they told us that the Scillies have no such season) but more often during the warmer months. The building is old and narrow, stands on a strip of land that used to be a garden, and the proprietor is David Pearson, a Derby man, who is also the island's social worker, a post he has held for thirty years.

The business began as a joint venture in Honiton a few years ago, with a stock of three thousand paperbacks, but Mr Pearson's partner dropped out and the transfer to St Mary's followed. In so limited a space the stock is necessarily small, but it is no longer restricted to paperbacks, and there is potential for variety, Mr Pearson referring to what he called "a Nissen hut in reserve". Conrad being a novelist of whom I wished to know more, I picked up a biography of him by Jocelyn Baines, who started his working life as an antiquarian bookseller.

There are no other second-hand bookshops in the Scillies, as far as I know, and bibliophiles looking for something bigger have to go to

Penzance, the nearest point on the mainland. Patricia Johnstone has a large general stock at Penzance Rare Books in Causewayhead.

Murray & Kennett, Horsham

My first job in Fleet Street, at the beginning of the 1960s, was with the *Daily Telegraph*, and Duff Hart-Davis's highly readable history of the paper, *The House the Berrys Built*, takes me back to my joyless time in the sub-editors' room. I had already read and admired it in hardback, and when I saw the softback in Murray & Kennett's shop in the Bishopric, I snapped it up at once.

One of the *Telegraph*'s countless editorial house-rules in those days was that any sum of foreign currency appearing in its columns had to be accompanied by the sterling equivalent in brackets. Hart-Davis, on the first page of his book, tells the story of Elizabeth Taylor arriving at Heathrow to recuperate after an illness and, on being asked how she felt, replying, "I'm feeling like a million dollars." Next day the *Telegraph* report rendered this as "I'm feeling like a million dollars (£357,000)." I wish I had kept my copy of the style-book in which that and all the other ridiculously inflexible rules were laid down as holy writ. Is it too much to hope that some day I might find one gathering dust in a second-hand bookshop?

John Murray, who used to be a teacher, and his mother, Muriel Kennett, opened the shop that bears their names in 1986, on a site previously occupied by a food and wine store called The Cellar and the Larder. There were two shops then, at numbers 100 and 102, but after Mrs Kennett died they were knocked together into one. Mr Murray's stock is crowded and interesting, ranging from religion (which had been Mrs Kennett's speciality) and philosophy to a hefty volume by Anna Ford on men. While I was browsing, a young couple came in to dispose of a box containing a large quantity of children's books, including *Beano* annuals and four Harry Potters. Mr Murray showed me this and wondered whether there was a family tragedy behind it.

Nearer the town centre, Tom Costin's Horsham Bookshop in Park

Place had another Fleet Street book, Philip Gibbs's *The Street of Adventure*, which was probably the first novel with journalism for its subject. On the whole newspaper life does not seem to lend itself to fictional treatment, and when journalists do appear in novels they are usually *cliché* characters, unhappily married and potential alcoholics; with those handicaps they could just as easily be estate agents or bookmakers. In films, too, newspapermen are nearly always unconvincing stereotypes. Arthur Christiansen, the Editor of the *Daily Express* in its heyday, was persuaded to play himself in *The Day the Earth Caught Fire*, but he sounded insipid – which he definitely wasn't. One critic wrote that the most dramatic thing he did was to take his spectacles off and put them on again.

I also connect Heathcote Williams's *The Speakers* with my early years in London and with the many Sundays I spent at Speakers' Corner listening to the best of those eloquent cranks. Williams, an Etonian, wrote it at the age of twenty-two and it was his first book. In Anthony Burgess's opinion, "This is a book that calls for no concessions, no patronising indulgence. It can stand quite confidently in the hard, Sophoclean light." Harold Pinter thought it "a remarkable achievement." And one of the speakers, William MacGuinness, said: "*The Speakers* is the only book worth reading since I myself wrote the Bible." I saw it in hardback in the Horsham Bookshop and for a moment was transported back to 1964, the year of its publication.

Seeing a biography of Maria Callas made me ponder the snob value of opera. Have you noticed that whenever some public figure wants to impress us with the breadth of his culture, he invariably refers to his opera-going habit? Never orchestral concerts or chamber music recitals; always opera. It will come as a shock to him to learn that the *Eroica* symphony is greater than any opera or oratorio.

Treasure Trove, Leicester

The Midlands is scarcely a happy hunting-ground for bibliophiles, but Sheppard's directory lists six second-hand shops in Leicester, which encouraged me to go and look. In the end I visited two, the

Treasure Trove and the Black Cat, and inexplicably failed to find a third, Maynard & Bradley, which is in Royal Arcade off Silver Street, in the overcrowded city centre; I saw every arcade except Royal. A businessman in his lunch hour went out of his way to help me, saying that he knew of Maynard & Bradley, but even he had to give up the search after much walking in circles.

The Treasure Trove is in Mayfield Road (turn left out of the railway station, walk up London Road, then go left again at the Victoria Park roundabout) and is owned by Linda Sharman, who used to teach physical education and special needs, and has always been interested in books. She first thought of starting a shop after reading the *Book and Magazine Collector* magazine, and realised this dream in 1993, on the premises of what had once been a firm of picture-framers.

As usual the subject of the internet came up, and Miss Sharman said: "It's been the saving of the shop and at least sixty per cent of our business is done on the internet now. I prefer finding and buying books through the traditional channels, but we have to be realistic."

The shop, where her brother Bill was at the receipt of custom the day I called, is on two floors, with a mezzanine landing containing a small selection of classics, plus stock by middle-of-the-road novelists like Daphne du Maurier and Jeffrey Farnol. I remember Farnol from my late 'teens and early twenties – historical romances such as *The Broad Highway* and *Beltane the Smith.* He is another of those authors I associate with the bridge period in my life between boys' and adult reading.

There is an outstanding children's section, with a rocking-horse in front of the shelves, and I investigated an 1889 reprint of the facsimile edition of *Tom Brown's Schooldays*, in which the author was given, not as Thomas Hughes, but as "An Old Boy." Seeing Edward Heath's book on sailing reminded me that Christopher Wordsworth, when he reviewed it in *The Observer* years ago, summed it up as "platitude and longitude."

Phil Woolley and his wife Karen run the Black Cat in Charles Street, having decided on that name because they are cat-mad and the initials come at the beginning of the alphabet, which is apparently useful for business purposes. Mr Woolley had a stall in the market before setting up shop. Nicola Howell, one of his assistants, told me that they do not stock anything antiquarian and specialise in crime fiction, children's stories, modern paperbacks by the likes of Ian Fleming and P. G. Wodehouse, and film books.

Early in my research for this book, I had a letter from the Reverend Prebendary Patrick Tuft in Chiswick, who wrote: "No story of the provincial bookshops in England would be complete without some account of a shop which existed in Leicester called Murray's. The street it was in was, I think, Loseby Lane, in the centre of the town not far from the cathedral church of St Martin. Although the name Murray was outside (and, curiously, the words Shakespeare's Head), the family who owned it was named Feaks. I got to know the shop when I was a schoolboy at the school by the cathedral. This was in the late 1940s.

"There were, in fact, two shops side by side. The main one had shelves of books opening onto the street and was dark and cavernous inside. When I first used to look in, it was still lit by gas and there was a fire blazing at the back of the shop behind a small counter. 'Old' Mr Feaks stood there. His son later took over and in the late forties electricity was introduced and shown off to the customers as if it were a recent invention.

"The other shop was locked and was perhaps a sort of storehouse. Upstairs it appeared not to have changed in generations. Of the stock I cannot now say. Mr Feaks complained that dealers from London would come and try to siphon off his best books.

"In later years the first shop was sold and the locked shop became the main one, the upstairs being a little tidied up. Later still, young Mr Feaks, now the only Mr Feaks, would sit in a large easy chair and, if there was cricket at Grace Road, just shut the shop and go to watch. Where the establishment first began and when it finally ended, I do not know."

Scarthin, Cromford

Scarthin Books was established by David Mitchell in 1974 and, in the words of its introductory leaflet, "has grown, free of plans, budgets and mission statements, into an eleven-roomed rainstorm refuge, where each subject (and staff member) competes for shelf space, and battles against the territorial ambitions of the café. Whatever your interests, there are likely to be hard-to-find books in this hard-to-find bookshop. They come not just from the international media conglomerates, but also from hundreds of smaller publishers in Britain, America, Europe and the Shetland isles."

Cromford is a few miles south of Buxton in the Peak District, and the shop, which overlooks a large pond beside The Promenade, opens seven days a week. Catering for what it calls "the majority of minorities", it houses at a very rough estimate forty thousand second-hand books and thirty thousand new ones; and having an interest in the weather more aesthetic than meteorological, I bought a Fontana paperback by Gordon Manley called *Climate and the British Scene*. It was first published in 1952, but that is almost irrelevant; the subject is dateless, like human nature.

As you have probably gathered, Scarthin is more than a shop, it is part of the community. The cafe serves organic food and can be hired for lectures and group meetings outside shop hours at low cost. Books are supplied to schools, colleges and libraries; the shop itself publishes titles of local interest such as *Family Walks*; and there are the now obligatory booksearch and internet adjuncts.

On a smaller scale, Buxton has an equally recommendable bookshop on the High Street, a short walk from the Opera House. This is Scrivener's, which is open seven days a week, with five floors, including a basement, holding a stock of thirty thousand volumes from pulp to antiquarian; bookbinding and restoration work is done on the ground floor at the front of the shop by Holly Serjeant and Janet Hopley.

Alastair Scrivener, who was born in Warwickshire, taught art in a Sheffield school before taking early retirement from the dispiriting paperwork of the job and going into bookbinding. From there it was a logical step to bookselling, which he finds fascinating. "You meet so many unusual and erudite people in it," he says. "And so many sad people as well." His stock is clearly laid out on shelves most of which he put up himself, and the children's room, complete with sofa, is particularly good (it is also used for Saturday coffee mornings).

Clifford Hubbard, who was a kennel lad during the 1920s, spent a lifetime working with and writing about dogs, and he opened the Doggie Hubbard Bookshop in Buxton in 1972 – possibly the only shop in the world to specialise in canine lore. At the time Mr Hubbard was nearing completion of a bibliography of dog books, his own collection alone running to fifteen thousand in twenty-eight languages. Later he and his Estonian wife Siri moved the shop to private premises in Aberystwyth, where he died at the turn of the century.

Rye Old Books

Aoife Coleman, a Dubliner who has lived in England since 1964, oversees Rye Old Books in Lion Street, in the town of Henry James and E. F. Benson, and she insists it is the oldest continually-trading second-hand bookshop there. It opened its doors in 1993, having previously been a pine shop; Miss Coleman herself became a bookseller after many years working as a health visitor, in north London and elsewhere. She told me about some of her cases, such as that of a family in Hastings who slept with their pet snakes.

Pinned up on a board just inside the entrance of her shop was something that in a way made me feel at home: a cutting from *The Times* of December, 1984, containing a review by Peter Ryde of a history of Rye Golf Club. Ryde succeeded the redoubtable Bernard Darwin as golf correspondent of the paper, and as a humble sub-editor regularly looking after his copy I got to know him well. Like Darwin, he was a versatile writer, able, when not skirting the fairways, to turn his hand to the light-hearted fourth leaders that used to be a feature of *The Times*, and, as a hobby, to the translation of books from the French.

Miss Coleman loves antiquarian books, with their beautiful

coloured plates, and as an example she showed me a copy of *Seats of the Noblemen and Gentlemen of Great Britain and Ireland*, by the Reverend F. O. Morris, published in Edinburgh *circa* 1880. It is, however, the kind of book all too often vandalised by unscrupulous people who cut out the plates, frame them, and sell them at a substantial profit. Nothing less than outrage is Miss Coleman's reaction to such practices.

Chapter and Verse, in the High Street, is one of the antiquarian shops admired by Miss Coleman. It has the authentic hush and polish, with the books, many of them behind glass, lovingly cared for and not cheap: the price range is ten pounds to fifteen thousand pounds. Spencer Rogers has owned the shop for five years, and altogether has been in the trade for a quarter of a century; before Rye he worked in Greenwich. His shop's motto is from St Thomas Aquinas: *Cavé librum unum habentem*, which translated means "Beware of the man with one book."

Clive Ogden, of the Meads Book Service in Lion Street, came into book dealing after a career embracing hotels, showbusiness, and much else. "Versatility is my middle name," he will tell you. His specialities include the Benson family, Ford Madox Ford, Edith Wharton, ghosts and topography. The Bookworm, opened in the High Street at Christmas, 2001, and run by Mike and Angela Kirkaldie, has an attractive stock in a small space but without room for expansion. Mrs Kirkaldie said they would like to branch out into the antiquarian field. Landgate Books, at Hilder's Cliff, was closed pending a change of ownership when I was in Rye, and Bill Menniss, the outgoing proprietor, had a notice on the door thanking his customers for five happy years.

D'Arcy Books, Devizes

We set off by road for Wiltshire at the same early hour of morning as England were starting their match with Brazil in the World Cup. This was a ruse to avoid any heavy traffic, and it worked. Two hours later we were approaching Devizes, the match was over, and by mere chance we learned the result at a butcher's shop where we called to ask something totally different from football.

Friends had grimaced when we said we were going to Devizes, but that may have had something to do with the fact that they did their army training there. We on the contrary rather took to the Georgian town, or at least to its central cluster of streets, and Drif in his day certainly took to d'Arcy Books in the High Street, describing it (according to a cutting on display beside the inquiry desk) as the most beautiful second-hand bookshop in Britain. It was founded in 1974 and the proprietors are Colin MacGregor, who specialises in militaria, and his wife Jenifer, who has a particular fondness for children's books. The whole stock, on two floors, is admirably representative, and the restful brown surroundings harmonise.

We climbed Pewsey Downs and gazed across Wiltshire before going on to Marlborough for the night. Anthony Spranger has an excellent shop there, in Kingsbury Street; William Golding, who had lived round the corner as a boy, wrote: "Our house was on the Green, that close-like square, tilted south." Mr Spranger said his shop was derelict when he took it over seven years ago, but it had been a bookshop twice before that. Business was improving little by little, year by year.

I made one of my unanticipated purchases here – the novelist Peter Vansittart's memoir *Paths From a White Horse*. An eclectic index is often enough in itself to make me buy a book of this type, and Vansittart's did just that, its cast of hundreds including R. M. Ballantyne, Neville Cardus, Dixie Dean, Sigmund Freud, Christ, Nietzsche, V. S. Pritchett, Philip Toynbee, Wagner, and T. C. Worsley. And I almost bought Hesketh Pearson's book about Boswell and Johnson, a work I did not know that prolific biographer had written.

The Katharine House Gallery on The Parade in Marlborough combines twentieth-century British art, antiques and books. Owned by Christopher Gange, it has been a going concern since 1983. The book stock has modern first editions, sport, history, poetry and the occult, but the outstanding feature is the Nevis railway collection, begun in 1987, which also contains reading matter of all kinds about trams, buses and canals. This is a shop to broaden the minds of all travellers by public transport.

On the other side of The Parade is the Military Parade Bookshop, run by the brothers Graham and Peter Kent since 1987. It is one small room crammed with books of naval, military and aviation history. "I read nothing but military books," Graham Kent told me – with a touch of exaggeration, perhaps? I remarked that Antony Beevor, with *Stalingrad* and *Berlin*, seemed to have cornered a market, and Mr Kent said: "He's a rich man now." I myself spent six months of my National Service in Berlin, in 1953, when the city was still half in ruins from the war. William Manchester is best-known for *The Death of a President*, which deals with the Kennedy assassination; the Kents' shop had *Goodbye, Darkness*, a harrowing account of Manchester's experiences as an infantryman in the Pacific war.

As we left Marlborough, my wife said that second-hand bookshops made her think of Battersea – "all those books sitting up like dogs begging to be found new homes."

Eric T. Moore, Hitchin

The Hitchin festival was on when I called at this shop in Bridge Street, which had a window display of crime fiction, including some of Dorothy L. Sayers's novels and a photograph of a letter (not easy to decipher despite being considerably enlarged) from Sayers to her publisher, Victor Gollancz. During the festival Christopher Dean, chairman of the Dorothy L. Sayers Society, gave a talk on the subject of "Dorothy L. Sayers, Lord Peter Wimsey and Hertfordshire" and Moore's sponsored it – a mark of the shop's importance to the town.

Eric Moore began his career as a commercial artist and changed to bookselling after the war. He worked for Hatchards in Piccadilly, and made an unsuccessful attempt to start a bookshop in Kensington, before opening the Hitchin business in 1963, on the site of an old inn. In 2000, when he was eighty-eight, he sold it to the brothers Paul and Mike Russell (the latter was born in Mr Moore's house), and they are now working hard to maintain a fine tradition.

There are two floors, ground and first, with thirty-five thousand volumes pleasantly arranged at reasonable prices, armchairs for long-term browsers among the lit. crit. shelves upstairs, maps and prints on the walls, and coffee and biscuits part of the service. Literary memorabilia can be seen in cabinets, where I noted a letter from Barbara Cartland, who lived in Hertfordshire, to Mr Moore. Altogether you feel that everything is as it should be in this shop.

An elderly lady, long retired from teaching German and Russian, had asked me to look out in the course of my travels for *The Puppet Show of Memory*, but she could not recall the author's name. A member of Moore's staff supplied the answer: Maurice Baring. The book was not in stock, however, and I bought, instead, *Three Men on the Bummel*, Jerome K. Jerome's sequel to his *Three Men in a Boat*, which has the Uncle-Podger-hanging-up-the picture episode that I once regarded as the funniest thing I had ever read. I have read Jerome's autobiography, and seen his play *The Passing of the Third Floor Back* performed by an amateur company in Notting Hill, but it is for *Three Men in a Boat* that he will be chiefly, if not solely, remembered.

Mr Moore has said: "I have been very fortunate with my assistants over the years. It has always been my policy to get to know them first as friends before offering them a job in the shop. Their expertise and loyalty are very much appreciated.

"I have also had one or two rather curious assistants. There was an unfrocked Anglican priest who became a fanatical Roman Catholic and caused havoc in the theology department by lowering the prices of my Anglican books, while the prices of my Catholic theology shot up in value.

"Although I have always looked on bookselling as a second best compared with my early ambition to become a successful artist, I have found the trade an amazingly varied pursuit which has satisfied my artistic and literary interests. In fact I would say that bookselling is the most humane, sociable, ill-organised, yet absorbing form of commerce to be found anywhere."

Elsewhere in Hitchin, The Bookbug, in The Arcade, has a paper-back-based stock, with hardbacks upstairs. Very different is Phillips of Hitchin (Antiques), which was established in 1884 and is housed in a redbrick Georgian building with a white porch in Bancroft. Jerome Phillips says it has what is probably the biggest collection in the world of books on furniture, but no general stock.

Barter Books, Alnwick

If you did not know the story already, the toy trains humming round the tops of the bookcases would give you a clue. For the building occupied by this very large and unusual second-hand bookshop in the Northumbrian town of Alnwick, midway between Newcastle and Berwick, was a grand Victorian railway station until becoming one of the many closed by Beeching forty years ago.

In 1991 Mary Manley, an American lady from Missouri, decided to open a bookshop, based on the swap system, called Barter Books. At her husband Stuart's suggestion, she did this in the front room of what was then his business manufacturing computer games on the site of the old station. They went into partnership, the bookshop grew and grew, and last year it attracted a quarter of a million visitors, many of them tourists rather than book-lovers, as Mr Manley concedes, but contributing to a remarkable figure nonetheless.

"We've got 400,000 books here," Mr Manley says. "There's a Barter Books at Seahouses but that's a separate concern and we only share the name. All the creative ideas here are my wife's - I just sell books."

Those "creative ideas" include the toy trains; printed quotations, hung between the bookcases, from such as Robert Frost, Jon Stallworthy, Ezra Pound and Baudelaire; a chess table in the old waiting-room ("men" obtainable from the reception desk); hot drinks and cookies awaiting the hungry browser just inside the main entrance; and pre-booked tours. By cosy association, a genuine coal fire, relic of the railway ticket office, helps to make the refreshments taste even better.

"Books and shops should be enjoyable - fun, if you like," Mr Manley goes on. "We have certain standards but we don't specialise. We like to think that some people may come in looking for a Mills &

Boon and go away with a Jane Austen. Some shops are elitist and unwelcoming. We try to make ours a pleasure to be in.

"The children's room can be wrecked on a daily basis but we don't mind. We accept that as an occupational hazard. Children are the readers of the future and they've got to be encouraged in the book habit as much as possible and offered an alternative to television."

Open seven days a week, the shop is on the main road into Alnwick off the A1, and well signposted, a luxury for a bookshop of any type. I dipped into *The Beauty of England*, by Thomas Burke (whose *Son of London* I bought in Hastings). He it seems saw little of beauty in Alnwick, but he would surely have liked Barter Books, even if it did replace the steam railway.

Farewell to True Bookshops

BY JOHN F. X. HARRIOTT

Not so many years ago I and a friend who is himself a considerable seller of books were tootling round the Lake District when we came by chance on the kind of secondhand bookshop which used to grace every town in the kingdom but is now as rare as a coach and four. Rooms of books unfolded one upon another, and staircases of books wound upwards into dark mysterious attics. There was that marvellous smell of cricket-bat oil and dusty bacon. We plunged inside like thirsty legionnaires at a waterhole. The bookseller sat in one of the rooms, at a vast desk, inspecting, almost motionless, what looked like the original Gutenberg Bible. He was ancient and sallow and far beyond any normal human intercourse. We crept about him silently, pulling out handfuls of ripe nineteenth- and twentieth-century first editions, old childhood favourites, books of Victorian instruction to prospective travellers abroad, and lowering to the floor tremendous theological tomes which took up the challenge at the end of St John's gospel. The floor was carpeted, so we were soundless; we spoke in signs and whispers.

Little by little I became aware that in all the soundlessness there was indeed a sound, the thinnest imaginable runnel of human speech – but coming from where? I followed the sound as best I could. It came from the area round the bookseller. I crept close. And there, by his elbow, behind a pile of books, was a radio, the volume pitched at the very extremity of hearing. I cocked an ear. By God, I thought, it sounds like a Test match commentary, and then, by God, it *was* the Test match commentary. Those poltergeist voices were Johnners, and Bailey, and Fred Trueman. I tried to catch the old man's eye. He scarcely blinked, or twitched a muscle; his breath would scarcely have stirred a candle-flame. A Buddha-like contentment suffused his parchment features, his mind was a hundred miles away. How could I get him to turn the volume up?

Conscious of the atmosphere, I tried to signal my needs by the subtlest of gestures: a slight movement of the head inside a rising bouncer, a delicate turn of the wrist à la Ranjitsinhji, an imitative padding up to kill the offbreak. At last the old man returned from wherever he was. The hooded eyes opened, the grey lips uttered. 'Do you want the cricket' he croaked. His hand stole out and turned up the knob on his wireless set. With a silent pantomime of thanks my friend and I seized armfuls of books and sank to the floor, there to turn pages and listen to the cricket. No other words were spoken. There was no need. It was a foretaste of paradise.

And there, sitting on the floor, I had a dream of paradise and a great shock it was. For on the instant, in a moment of insight, I realised that I was not hungry for the kingdom so as to unlock the mystery of the Trinity. My paradise was very earthy. It was being able to watch all the great cricketers since time began, to drink all the great clarets since time began, to read all the great books since time began, and to listen to all the great wits since time began. And to do these things with the people one most loved with intervals for music.

Good old bookshops kindle such thoughts. The new bookshops and especially the newest of all bookshops which sell nothing but piles of ill-written, ill-spelled, ill-bound non-books from America, offer neither welcome nor aura. They do not invite one to buy good books because they are cheap, but to buy books simply because they are cheap. Such shops have no dark corners, no winding staircases, no smell of antiquity, no ripening booksellers or collectors poring over their catalogues. Instead they have neon lights and rows of paperbacks in alphabetical order and a computer to tell the customer that everything worth reading is out of print. They are savage places where there is always a keening wind and moans of spiritual hunger troubling the air.

The books these places advertise in lurid boxes and packets are also exceedingly horrible. Most are untouched by human hand and written to a formula, apparently by the same machine. Very many seem to have been subsidised by the CIA and the Mossad – the Israeli intelligence service – for their heroes and their values are mainly drawn from these. An almost equal number come out under the names of ageing actresses with souls as empty as the Gobi desert. And a third category have no conceivable purpose or relationship with proper books but are merely vehicles to carry a dust cover offering a free portrait of some *ersatz*, transient television personality. As Colonel Sanders products are to real chicken, as McDonald's french fries are to real chips, as the US government is to real statesmen, so are these emporia to real bookshops and the objects they sell to real books. Somewhere in London there should be a Wailing Wall for those who love books and bookshops, and now feel abandoned, and better still a place of execution for the publishers who have sold their temples for bathing huts on the beach.

This article first appeared in *The Tablet*, the national Catholic weekly, to whom I am indebted for permission to reproduce it here.

Index